HOW TO PREDICT THE WEATHER WITH A CUP OF COFFEE

HOW TO PREDICT
THE WEATHER WITH A
CUP OF COFFEE

AND OTHER TECHNIQUES FOR
SURVIVING THE 9–5 JUNGLE

BY MATTHEW COLE

Collins

First published in 2010 by Collins

HarperCollins *Publishers*
77–85 Fulham Palace Road
London W6 8JB

www.harpercollins.co.uk

1 3 5 7 9 10 8 6 4 2

Text © Matthew Cole 2010
Illustrations © Nick McFarlane 2010

The author asserts his moral right to
be identified as the author of this work.

A catalogue record for this book
is available from the British Library.

ISBN: 978-0-00-731508-6

Printed and bound in Great Britain
by Clays Ltd, St Ives plc.

FSC is a non-profit international organisation established
to promote the responsible management of the world's forests.
Products carrying the FSC label are independently certified
to assure consumers that they come from forests that are managed
to meet the social, economic and ecological needs
of present and future generations.

Find out more about HarperCollins and the environment at
www.harpercollins.co.uk/green

Certain activities in this book (you'll spot them) bring with them the
possibility of injury, illness, loss or embarrassment. But all adventure has
an element of risk and it would be wrong to miss out on any of it, so please exercise
common sense and take all necessary care when performing any of the activities
included (and if you are a child under 16 always ask a grown-up for help).
Rest assured that any risk arising from these activities is all yours.

The author and the publishers do not accept any responsibility for any harm
that may occur from your decision to follow the instructions contained in this book.

CONTENTS

ABOUT THE AUTHOR

Matthew Cole is a television producer who loves to write books. He lives in Bristol with his wife and their two children. He has a black belt in building flat-pack furniture and in his spare time restores antique metronomes.

ACKNOWLEDGEMENTS

With thanks to Mum, especially for recalling every detail of the M1 windscreen-wiper episode.

Thanks to Denise Bates, Martin Toseland and Helena Nicholls.

Also to Jon 'Leatherman' Riley, Ewen Thomson and Lofty Wiseman, who all inspired bits of this book without knowing it.

And finally, thanks to Joanna for lots of things, especially for her leniency over the smells from the car engine and any other mishaps (known or unknown).

PROLOGUE

We were under a motorway bridge to get out of the rain and Dad came out with his favourite phrase: 'We'll rig something up, son.' I was about eight, I think. We were on a family trip to London and the windscreen wipers had just given out. 'We'll rig something up,' he said, and that's what he did. Twenty minutes later we were back on the M1 southbound with the wipers flip-flopping across the windscreen. It's just that this time they were powered by a length of string fed into both back windows. My brother and I pulled as my sister called time.

As a feat of engineering this wasn't much to shout about. But that's not the point. Some string and a few knots had changed our world. Out of a crisis we'd conjured an adventure. We now had windscreen wipers with voice-operated variable speed control, and it felt good.

Dad was like a lot of dads back then; they had DIY in their DNA. They'd take a car engine to bits on the drive and collect miscellaneous odds and ends in jam jars (typically Araldite and string, batteries and radio parts, curtain hooks and electrical solder). Dad even had an extra special premium selection in his bedside drawer, a shrine to his life's big purpose: fixing things.

There'd be no point trying to emulate these old-fashioned can-do dads today; they'd been schooled since childhood in improvisation and making do. When their bikes got a puncture they didn't use a tyre lever to ease the tyre off the rim; they used a spoon. Dad's puncture kit was three spoons wrapped in an oily rag, like a mechanic's wedding present. By the time they had kids of their own these dads could wrestle a tyre off a bicycle wheel with their bare hands. They were masters of the universe, lord of all physical forces, and they could fix anything, all before teatime too.

When I became a dad I felt I should get a piece of the same kind of action. I dabbled a bit; I had my own collection of Ikea spanners and kept a small screwdriver and a key for bleeding the radiators tucked away in my socks drawer. But this was small time. Really there's no way in the world I was going to spend a precious Saturday stripping down a carburettor or build a collection of washers that would fill several jam jars. It just wasn't me. So I found myself thinking back, rerunning my all-time favourite Dad story. And looking again at what happened on that rainy motorway, the answer struck me, like a piece of self-help from the days before airbags.

You see, although the wipers were working again, Dad hadn't really *fixed* anything. He'd just side-stepped the problem. Armed with nothing but a ball of string, he showed the world who was boss. The message was clear: make stuff happen, and if it happens to you first then do something back. Oh, and keep a ball of string handy at all times.

Dad's rigged-up contraption had led me into the territory where simple always wins. In the age of digits and downloads here's a place where avoirdupois and analogue still hold sway, where a father and son can reconnect to the big stuff that controls our universe. The tricks and dodges in this book are my personal doorway into this Lost World.

Come and join me in the land where string is king.

THE PARABLE OF THE IPOD AND THE ONION

It was a huge viral video hit. People couldn't get enough. It showed you how a guy had charged his iPod by sticking the USB recharger in an onion left overnight in some Gatorade (a lurid blue 'sports drink'). That's bloody brilliant, I thought. So did thousands of others. It felt fabulous. It was a huge hit. Most views of the week. Hey everyone! You can charge your iPod with a vegetable! Onions 1, Apple Inc. 0.

But something didn't add up. It doesn't work.

Initially this is disappointing news. But what really matters is the groundswell of glee that greeted the very idea. Gatorade contains 'electrolytes', so it had a ring of credibility. Sticking a USB connector into an onion, though? Do you really think so? 'Course not. Yet, logic aside, tens of thousands of people were prepared to believe. It was an article of faith.

What this reveals is a longing for an elemental simplicity to deliver us from all of life's frustrating fiddly bits. We want muddy truth to triumph over the modern world's incomprehensible complexity. This book offers some suggestions as to how it can. Only none of them involve an onion; sorry . . .

INTRODUCTION

Warning! This is a guide to survival in the real world. That's the world you see when you step out of the lift at Ikea. It's not a place where penknives, compasses or the rubbing together of sticks are particularly appropriate. And the eating of bugs and leaves would be just . . . stupid.

Whatever you've been told, our ancestors didn't develop their skills of survival so that they could stay alive in the woods. They had other plans. They wanted to move into a city, buy a car and install sat nav.

How to Predict the Weather with a Cup of Coffee celebrates what happens once they got there and man's native instincts came to town. It revives some of the tricks from our primitive past and unleashes our flair for survival on a nasty new threat: all of life's tedious bits. I see this as a shot of red-blooded purpose into our pale urban backsides, turning the 9–5 into a non-stop adventure.

Some of the tricks and dodges in these pages are nicked from the Neolithic hunter; some are purloined from the pocket book of the Victorian explorer and some you already do every day. I call it 'Urban bushcraft' and it's an art and a science that's been in development ever since we had Neanderthals for neighbours. A lot has happened since then, so here's a quick recap.

OK, this is how it goes.

First there is this ape. He walks out of the forest, gets into some basic grooming and the result, eventually, is you. You're the slickest life-form to wear a loincloth and you can turn your hand to anything. With your super-sized brain and those freaky opposable thumbs you know what you want, and you know how to get it.

You clock up seven or eight millennia of breakneck progress, plus a few more when (frankly) you're just coasting. You rise above every challenge you face with boundless ingenuity. You get better and better at everything, and as a result you have less and less to do. Sod this hunting business, let's start a farm. Fed up with building shelters? Let's get into property development. These buttons are a bit fiddly, what about a zip?

And suddenly, you've cracked it. Survival is in the bag; shrink-wrapped, bar-coded and scanned. Bleep! Do you need any help packing today, sir?

Now, just hold it there a second. This bit's important. Don't worry, you've got a moment while you swipe your card.

Think back a few thousand years. You've just tracked your first antelope and you're standing there, spear cocked, all ready to turn it into lunch. Imagine how that felt. Now look at yourself. Instead of a blood-splattered spear and a steaming great antelope you've got a PIN number and a carrier bag of groceries. Different isn't it?

What you may have just experienced as you compressed ten thousand years of human experience into one supermarket second is *the niggle*. It's that little larva of doubt worming in somewhere round the back. Welcome to the modern world; this is what it's like, I'm afraid. In theory things are great, all urges are satisfied and all needs are met. But there's something missing: excitement. Oh, that reminds me – don't forget to buy yourself a scratchcard.

HARDWIRED AS CAVEMEN

When our brains were hardwired the job description was just one word: survive. Back then, life was in the balance every day. Sundays and bank holidays included.

But times changed and so did the priorities. We used to have to know when to hunt and when to run away, but now we just need to know which day to put the bins out. We're programmed for cut and thrust, a 24-7 existence that's contested tooth and claw, not a 9–5 working day with occasional tea and biscuits.

Of course, all this lying around not doing much is great, in theory. The problem is 'the niggle'. This is worth going into, because if nothing else it explains why you get such a kick out of lighting the barbecue.

Our primal urges, you'd think, cover a pretty straightforward shopping list: hunger, shelter, warmth . . . done. But there's one more evolution has armed us with. It's the urge to feel the thrill that come with satisfying all the other urges. That rush of bringing home the bacon is a reward in itself. In the 1960s, psychologists would have called that a bio-feedback loop. To you and me it's a vicious circle and, because of it, we're completely snookered.

Our DNA tells us to look for the kicks we got from all the big bad dangerous stuff that we just don't have to do any more. And now, like a dog chasing rabbits in its sleep, we can't stop. As you stand at the barbecue and smell the fat fizzing on the charcoal you're acting out your favourite flashback. Man make fire! Cook, eat . . . yum! And you can't switch this stuff off. It took a few million years to develop this baby. Get used to it, it's yours to keep.

If your life is spent going undercover behind enemy lines or hunting grizzlies from a log cabin beside the Yukon this may not apply. Life may be exciting enough. But for the rest of us there's the niggle. No wonder we get a bit ratty from time to time.

THE KEYS TO THE FERRARI

THE BEAR NECESSITIES

Over the centuries we've got very good at keeping our caveman brain quiet by throwing it a bone now and then. It's what the entertainment industry has been doing for centuries. Movies are fantasy workouts for the primal self. They fall into two camps.

First there's the Back to Eden fantasy, the one where the caveman gets to go home and lead a simple life, just as Nature intended . . . It's *Treasure Island* or *Robinson Crusoe*, *The Waltons*, *Survivor* and *Lost*. This is powerful stuff. Has anyone ever watched *The Jungle Book* and actually wanted our man-cub hero Mowgli to go back and live in the man village?

The other kind of caveman fantasy is where the savage inside us gate-crashes the modern world. It's why *Basic Instinct* was the best ever title for a movie, and why Shoot 'em up games take over the male mind. It's all chewing gum for our instinctive self, which explains that odd sense of calm that comes over you on walking out of a slasher movie. Chase scenes do the same job too; deep down we recognise how it feels to be the prey, whether playing chase in the playground or being hunted down by a robotic Terminator for the tenth time on DVD. It gives us the chance to rehearse it all again. And inside we squeal with pleasure.

Now we come to the fun part. It's like discovering a Ferrari sitting in your garage. Or if you're not that into cars, it's where you find out you have a secret talent for wiggling your ears . . . whichever you prefer.

Your instinctive self is a highly tuned and finely calibrated piece of evolutionary engineering, but for most of the week you just leave it in the garage. We're compelled to keep this powerful machine a secret from the civilised world. The urge comes over us in two ways:

1. We think if we give in to instinct we'll start turning up at meetings with wild staring eyes and custard stains down our front. So we just don't talk about it, we pretend it's not there. It's the woolly mammoth in the room.

2. We treat instinct like a hyperactive dog. It can be kept locked inside as long as you give it a run at evenings and weekends, whether it's a fight club, manoeuvres with the Territorial Army, or working through the complete airport novels of the Bravo Two Zero veterans.

But of all the occasional outings for our instinct, one type stands out head and shoulders above the rest, loud and proud in khaki shorts, hiking boots and obligatory fleece. Yes, it's time to throw out the deodorant and head for the woods to learn about survival skills. Under the watchful gaze of men with long knives and a faraway look in their eye you get to skin rabbits and distil your pee into drinking water.

For millions of men this stuff is an outlet for pent-up frustrations; it's a secret ventilation shaft from the soul through which the inner caveman gets to emerge into the outside world. And of course, it's an insurance against the collapse of global civilisation, when the ability to track hedgehogs and signal in semaphore would be quite handy.

But what if the closest you come to a desert in your day-to-day life is a square mile with no cash machine, and the highest summit you've seen today is the top of the multi-storey? Why escape to a fantasy wilderness to get our primal rocks off? Why not use all our innate brilliance to generate some red-blooded adventures right here, in the 9–5, where it matters most?

It's time for bushcraft to come out of the woods. It's just as much fun, far more relevant, and there's no vague whiff of urine.

Man loves to make a good fire. But why persist with sticks and fire lighters when you can use a car battery and a Brillo Pad, with far more impressive results?

Navigation used to be about reading the stars and finding the campsite. For the urban bushman it's about direction finding by Sky dish, and finding where on earth you parked the car.

And here's the best bit. Urban bushcraft doesn't mean turning your back on the comfort of central heating, wireless broadband and a fridge full of cold drinks.

There's a lot to learn. Let's get started.

SURVIVAL V BUSHCRAFT

They have different dress codes, different terminology and different attitudes to fossil fuels. But the main difference goes a little deeper.

Our fascination with bushcraft sprang from a revival of interest in American 'Wildwood Wisdom' and Australian aboriginal skills, shortly after World War Two, when it offered some simple certainty in an uncertain world.

Back then you cooked up your coffee on the embers every night and a man's best friend was his gun and coon-skin hat. Now there's a Starbucks on every corner and a man's only friend is his iPhone. But like the woodsman, the urban bushman's aim is to be happy and relaxed in his chosen habitat. After all, it's a nice place to be.

How to light a fire

a) Bushcraft   b) Survival

You've heard of bushcraft before, I'm sure. But you may have noticed that there are lots of people doing the same kind of stuff, but calling it survival. Which is which? Here's a quick and easy identification guide.

BUSHCRAFT	SURVIVAL
TROUSERS	
Shorts. If too small then probably Australian (but that's ok, they invented all this stuff).	Long trousers. Gore-Tex and camo gear. Stubble.
DEMEANOUR	
Relaxed, like big boy scouts. Keen to give it all an educational purpose. They like to be at one with their environment.	All very breathless and fast paced. This lot just want to survive and get the hell home, quick. Whatever it takes.
FIRE	
Natural firelighting techniques. They like bow drills.	Oil from the Zippo, petrol from a wrecked car.
DIET	
Nuts, leaves, wild game, witchetty grubs.	Very happy to snare game, skin rabbits. But prefer to stick to ration packs.
SOURCES	
Ancient wisdom and primitive tribes. Especially aboriginal Australians.	Once knew someone in the SAS. Also respected: Royal Marines, US Navy Seals and French Foreign Legion.

1.
THE INDOOR BUSHMAN

Most survival guides would leave you politely at your front step, on the presumption that if you're home then you're safe. But for us it's indoors that it all begins. The reason's simple: the urban bushman is driven to unearth new challenges and new thrills in the most familiar of places, and, for that, there's no place like home.

With this fresh perspective and a few new tricks, your humble abode will be transformed into the Great Indoors; a place that screams adventure, with its wide expanse of carpet, and seductive line-up of gadgets (just look at all those remote controls!), not to mention the benefit of central heating and more tea than you could ever drink.

It falls naturally into two sections. To begin, this chapter concentrates on handy skills to turn everyday annoyances at home into a journey of discovery; junk calls, washing up and arguments over the telly are all problems we're out to solve.

But there's another important dimension to bushcraft with your slippers on, far beyond pure practicalities. Home is a place of respite from the need for results that muscles in on the rest of your life. So in the second part of this chapter you'll find some bushcraft for the weekend, where we take things at a more leisurely pace. There are discoveries to share with the family and suggestions to ensure you'll always have something to do when it's raining.

But first, it's purely practical. You need to put the kettle on, so let's start in the kitchen.

SCREENING CALLS WITH A MICROWAVE

If you've ever felt that your mobile rules your life, this one's for you; a guaranteed way to dodge unwanted calls.

HOW TO SCREEN YOUR CALLS WITH A MICROWAVE

This stems from one big difference between two gadgets that use microwaves. In order to communicate, the mobile phone gets microwaves to shoot around, passing through anything in the way, whether it's solid brick or gooey grey matter. Our microwave cookers, on the other hand, prefer to contain the waves and focus them on a single bowl of porridge. The microwave stops them escaping with a Faraday cage (a mesh in which the holes are too small for microwaves to squeeze through).

So when your phone rings and you suspect it's someone you'd rather avoid, here's what to do:

1. Start to move towards the microwave (switched off).
2. Answer brightly, 'Hello . . .'
3. Gradually move your phone in and out of the oven and watch the signal strength fall and rise. With the phone

held in the oven (keep the oven switched off, of course)
you lose contact completely. Just inside the open door,
it fades in and out.

4. Now assume a confused voice . . . 'Sorry I'm losing you,
we're going through a tunnel' . . . etc.

The strength of this system is that it can be used after you've answered; far more convincing than hanging up in mid-call. After a couple of tries you'll become a virtuoso, bringing the caller in and out of range at will, playing them like a fish on a hook; then, just as they think they've got you back . . . you've gone for good. (NB. Also works with wireless landline phone, though harder to get away with.)

Remember not to shut the door completely – that dinging sound is a giveaway.

THE TOP FIVE ITEMS REGULARLY MICROWAVED IN THE NAME OF ENTERTAINMENT

First the microwave cooker brought us the TV dinner, then it made it possible for generations of boys to blow up ping-pong balls and experiment on M&Ms. Now the two have converged to such a degree that there are people sitting down with a ready meal to watch a cable channel devoted to putting everyday objects inside a microwave.*

1. Ping-Pong ball	*the original and the best*
2. Soap	*a volcano of lather*
	solidifying into a
	surreal sculpture
3. CDs	*a circular light storm*

---

* I recommend *Is It a Good Idea to Microwave This?* – the Californian show with the billing 'Twice a week, our microwave specialists microwaves different objects . . . so you don't have to!'

4. Light bulb/strip-light tube   *and there was light . . .*
                                        then a bang
5. M&Ms/marshmallows/grapes   *gooey pyrotechnics*

CALLING ALL MICROWAVES

If I said that you can cook popcorn with the signal from your mobile phone would you believe me? Not strong enough? Then how about with ten mobile phones? If the idea seems to make sense it's because of an in-built assumption that follows from the knowledge that mobiles communicate using microwaves. The very word conjures up images of piping hot ready meals, doors that go ping and a lot of 1970s science about cooking from the inside. But today's communication microwaves (the ones that allow you to share ringtones with your Facebook friends in Kuala Lumpur) aren't the same as the microwaves in the cooker (the ones that heat a lasagne in one minute). You can't cook with mobile phones any more than you can phone someone via the defrost setting.

The microwave cooker was invented by US radar engineer Percy Spencer after he realised that his bar of chocolate had been mysteriously melted in the lab. He decided to experiment and went out and bought some popcorn kernels. As they popped all over his workbench Percy had his eureka moment and snacked on the first ever microwave popcorn. That was 1945, and popcorn is still the world's favourite microwave food. I've always wondered how he knew.

Handy places to find microwave ovens are:

- service stations
- train buffet cars
- professional kitchens
- local authority tips – salvage one as a phone screen to install at home

MICROWAVE SAFETY TEST WITH A MOBILE

Turn what you've learned on its head for a quick and easy safety test for your old microwave. You'll want to run this check every day – if only to show off how clever you are.

You need a mobile phone, a microwave and another phone (landline will do fine). Check your mobile has a signal, place it in the oven, shut the door and call it up. You should find you go straight to answer machine, because the microwaves can't reach the phone. If it rings it means the microwaves can get in and that means you've got problems, because if the waves can get in, they can get out as well. Watch out for your eyes. It stings when they start to cook.

THE FREEZER FIGHTS BACK

HOW TO FIX YOUR HARD DISK AMONG THE FROZEN PEAS

Compared with the microwave the fridge and the freezer are the old timers in your kitchen, still running on technology barely changed since the 1940s. Of all your white goods this pair are the oldies, humming quietly to themselves, barely noticed. So it's especially pleasing to be able to help them get one over on new technology.

'The click of death' is the name sci-fi-obsessed tekkies give the sound a computer's hard disk makes when it can't retrieve any data, and it usually means that it's time to panic. On hearing it, your palms go clammy, the blood drains from your head and, when people ask 'Did you save it anywhere else?', you have to fight the temptation to scream. In all cases of panic, the advice is always do something, anything; make a cup of tea, dig a hole, bake some bread. Well, I'd suggest what you do is put your hard drive in the freezer; it will keep you busy *and* it could just help.

Fridges and freezers are sealed by a magnetic strip running around the inside of the door. That's why you need to give it that extra little tug when you open it. Have a look – it's obvious when you know it's there. You can use it to slip little notes underneath for the next person to open the fridge, or to magnetise a pin and make a homemade compass. And when it comes to sorting the recycling it's a handy helper for telling aluminium cans from steel. Aluminium won't stick to the magnet, but steel will.

WARNING! This is a last resort that may not work. I offer it to you in the knowledge that it's helped many people before, and that right now you'll try anything.
ANOTHER WARNING!! This can get quite technical, but the urban bushman isn't one to shirk the challenge of reading an instruction manual or downloading a help page or two.

Day one

- Remove your hard drive (if you don't know how, you'll find instructions easily enough on the web. Look for them before you start pulling your computer apart).
- If you can, fit a USB connector into the drive (unless you're an IT champion you'll need help . . . which means more web surfing). This just helps you to hook up your drive very quickly, but it's not essential.
- Vacuum seal it in a 'zip-lock'-type bag as best you can.
- Leave it in the freezer for a few days (this isn't a precise science, some people find a few hours is long enough).

A few days later

When the big day comes, be prepared to retrieve as much of the data as you can very quickly (freezing is only ever a temporary fix).

- Take your drive out of the freezer. If you wired up a USB connector into the computer, plug it straight in. Otherwise reinstall in the usual way. Use an ice-pack or freezer block to keep it cool.
- Start to search for the drive and open the media. Muttering 'C'mon, c'mon' usually helps here too.
- If the click of death is replaced by the ping of hope don't start to celebrate until you've transferred everything to another disk. Start with the most essential stuff first.
- All copied? Now you can celebrate!

How it works

When you kick the telly it's because you know just enough to think it could work; if it does though, you haven't got the foggiest notion why. This is a bit like that; I see it as old-fashioned physics administering a gentle slap to a technological young upstart.

There are two plausible theories as to what's going on:

1. *The mechanical theory*: it could be that the 'read' head of the drive is jammed, and that freezing makes the metal parts shrink just enough to free it for a few minutes.
2. *The magnetic theory*: hard drives store information magnetically and the magnetic field gets stronger as the recording media get colder, allowing the drive to read it more easily.

Oh, and before you shut the freezer, you may as well get out a frozen lasagne … it's time for dinner.

DISHWASHER COOKERY

This is perfect if you can't face doing any washing up after you've cooked. The longest cycle on the machine (usually 90 minutes or so) will cook fish and vegetarian foods perfectly well, while you process a load of dishes at the same time.

The dishwasher chef's primary skill is wrapping up each dish in a watertight little parcel of foil. The key here is to make sure the foil is tightly sealed so no water can get in and ruin your food. It's a skill that will come in handy later (see Car-engine cookery). An easier cop out here is to seal it all up in a freezer bag.

POACHED, STEAMED AND GLEAMING SALMON STEAKS

There's no limit on space (unless, of course, you already have a fairly full machine), so go for broke with some big meaty salmon steaks.

Serves four

Cooking time: 70 minutes

Ingredients:

- Four large salmon steaks
- Seasoning
- Cooking foil

Steps:

1. Season each steak and wrap with dill and lemon inside a foil parcel with tightly crimped edges. If you're using detergent in the wash cycle, consider sealing the salmon inside a freezer bag.
2. Place parcels on the top shelf and set dishwasher to its highest and longest setting. A 2–3cm-thick steak will cook to pink perfection in a 70-minute hot cycle.

DISHWASHER LASAGNE

Serves four

Cooking time: 1 hour

Ingredients:

Use a recipe of your choice for vegetarian ricotta or spinach lasagne.

Steps:

1. Make the lasagne in the middle of a large sheet of foil, building up layers of pasta and filling as you go.

2. Wrap lasagne securely in the foil.

3. Place the package flat on the bottom rack of the dishwasher.

4. Set to the normal wash cycle and repeat if necessary until cooking time is reached.

5. Before serving, leave the lasagne to stand for five minutes.

A genuine benefit of dishwasher cookery is that you're far less likely to burn your dinner. But sometimes it's going to happen, and when it does the urban bushman knows exactly whom to turn to . . .

SLUG SKIVVIES

RECRUIT YOUR GARDEN SLUGS TO DO THE CHORES

For centuries ancient tribes have cooperated with animals for mutual benefit, whether it's working with dogs in the hunt, following birds to a source of water or using maggots to clean wounds. Now we can translate this tradition to the urban environment, calling on the expertise of some back-garden wildlife to help with some particularly dull chores.

Back-garden pot washers

Burned-on food gunk is the last thing you want to face on a Sunday night after a particularly good lasagne or nut roast. When your scourers have turned black and the dishwasher won't shift it, here's what to do: forget washing up, just pop it outside overnight and let the slugs go to work.

Slugs are equipped with 27,000 tiny teeth spaced along a rasping tongue-like appendage called a radula. It's custom-made to get into small gaps and crevices and scrape off rich sources of food, like mould (or burned-on cheese bake). They really are specialists at this.

TIPS

- Slugs follow habitual trails, so for a better chance of success put your pots on a slime line. If they don't finish it off in one sitting, they'll be back.
- Place pots upside down (leaving a gap for slug access) and wash before re-use.

Cleaning grout the organic way

Black mould on the grout between your bathroom tiles is a sad inevitability of modern life – where there's moisture there's mould. But one thing's for certain: you need to get that off before the parents/in-laws come to visit. It can be a devil of a job too, unless you recruit the assistance of that supremely equipped mould-muncher, the slug.

You'll need to find a few slugs and familiarise them with the new environment on the tiles before they do much cleaning. Give them a dark damp hideaway where they can spend the day, making sure they can get out. They prefer to work at night so be prepared for a shock if you like a shower after dark.

If you get the timing of this right, the slugs munch away on the mould all night, leaving you with spotless, if slightly slimy, grout. The great benefit of course is that it's entirely free from nasty detergents or cleaners.

It can take a while, so be patient and if there's no improvement after a few days, consider changing your slugs.

THE WEEKEND BUSHMAN

Now that your chores are done it's time to focus on something more edifying: bushcraft that soothes the soul, especially designed to fill up your weekend or while away an evening in or crafty morning off.

I'll start with a favourite demonstration of the mood-altering possibilities of bushcraft in the home.

HOW TO TURN YOUR TV INTO A COSMIC TIME MACHINE

This is a cure for a condition commonly known as 'Nothing on the Telly'. When we complain that 'nothing's on' what we mean is that there's nothing that's going to grab us by the scruff of the neck, slap us on both cheeks and demand our attention. Well if that's the case, then this will fix it.

Here's how to use your television to pick up a 13.7 billion-year-old signal from outer space, in three easy steps.

1. Turn on telly.
2. Unplug satellite or cable box, unplug aerial.
3. Stare at static.

That 'snow' or static is background 'noise' generated by the soup of radio waves washing around the earth. When you're tuned to *Coronation Street*, the signal is so strong you don't see the noise. But when the telly has nothing else to latch on to it tries to translate the 'noise' into a picture, and 'snow' or 'static' is the result. Now turn up the sound and listen, because here comes the good bit . . .

Most of this static is caused by the radio and TV signals that are constantly buzzing around the world, Chinese minicabs, Somali weather men, Russian tank commanders. During the Battle of the Atlantic in World War Two a young telegraphist on a Royal Navy cruiser picked up what he thought was a coded signal from a nearby German U-boat. Out there in the Atlantic they tended to think about U-boats quite a lot. Nobody could understand the message or even recognise the code. The report was duly sent back to Liverpool to be pored over by the experts, who couldn't understand how this message had come to be received in mid-Atlantic. It wasn't any code or language they recognised. Then, eventually, its origin was tracked down. It was a short-range transmission from a Russian tank commander in Stalingrad, appearing as bright as you like thousands of miles away at sea. This is a shining example of the erratic behaviour of radio waves and their tendency to pop up all over the place, a syndrome known as analogous propagation.

But 1 per cent of the noise that you're seeing (and hearing) is something else; it's the radiation left over from the event that gave birth to the entire universe, it's the receding echo of the Big Bang, now showing on your very own TV.

I'll pause here while you take in the enormity of what you're looking at. Now stare at the screen again. One per cent of that fizzing energy and activity is coming to you from something that happened more than 13 billion years ago.

For me this is a bit like smelling salts: you can use it to snap you out of any mood, at any time. And that's not the end of it; the explanation of how we know all this is pretty good too.

How it works

If we'd always had digital tellies we'd never have seen this phenomenon. But in the old days of analogue, TV had to pick up a wide range of frequencies, and this microwave echo of the Big Bang – gradually fading as it spreads through our ever-expanding universe – just happens to overlap into the same range, so our tellies were able to see it. Its proper name is Cosmic Background Radiation (CBR). It's on the radio too, somewhere in all that white noise between stations.

CBR was found by a pair of American physicists in the 1960s. They were trying to listen to the stars and were getting increasingly irritated by a constant noise on their super-powerful receiver. At first they thought it might be caused by pigeon poo on their dish, but they had it cleaned and it was no different. Then they wondered if it could be radiation from nearby New York, but they pointed their dish the other way and it was still there. Eventually they found it wasn't even coming from within the galaxy, but was present everywhere, throughout the universe. Then they looked at each other and realised what it must be. They had found what's left of the heat from the Big Bang.

SOFA SCIENCE LESSON

Whenever kids complain there's nothing on, then, seize the chance to grab their attention by turning the TV into a cosmic data receiver. Relating it to *Star Wars* in some way might help too, depending on the demographics. But get it in while you can; before long all TVs will have built-in digital tuners, and it will be much harder to tune into the cosmos by just tuning out.

FORECAST THE WEATHER WITH INTERFERENCE

Once the whole Big Bang thing has sunk in, there's still more to be done with the static on your out-of-tune radio and telly. This time, your TV is being turned into a weather detector, on the lookout for extreme events in the atmosphere.

ANALOGUE REVIVAL

To pick up the weather you need to be able to tune into the lower end of the VHF (very high frequency) band. This used to be packed with TV channels, but now they've mostly moved up to UHF (ultra high frequency), with the lower frequencies being phased out.

And now the onset of digital TV means that all analogue signals, even the

UHF stuff, will be switched off, and new TVs won't be equipped to tune into these analogue signals at all. This means that anyone with a brand new digital TV is going to miss out. It's only a minor tragedy though; you can always go and dig the old set out of the attic. And if you haven't got yourself a new set just yet, what better excuse to stick with what you've got.

Just because TV's going digital, the laws of physics have no plans to follow suit, so these weather events are going to be on the same part of your dial for years to come.

LIGHTNING STORM ON YOUR TV

As soon as you hear thunder, get ready to catch a spectacular lightning storm on TV.

You need to be able to tune your TV to somewhere around 55 MHz. In the USA this is where you still find Channel 2. Some French channels broadcast on it too, but in the UK it hasn't been used since the 1980s. None of that matters, of course, if you can tune it in manually.*

It helps to turn the brightness right down until you have no picture. When lightning strikes nearby it will throw bands of light across the screen, getting bigger the closer it gets.

This used to be a popular way to look out for tornadoes in America's tornado alley (tornadoes are accompanied by lightning but also generate a signal themselves). So if your set does suddenly brighten for more than a few seconds at this frequency, and you can't see lightning, it could well be there's a twister coming in. Time to head for the cellar!

---

* Manual tuning: 55 MHz is a very low frequency for TV signals, but most pre-1990 TVs can reach down that far. If you're a hoarder and still have a pre-1990s black and white set, then there's a good chance that it was always tuned in to 55Mhz, so it may need no retuning. Push-button sets normally have a tuning wheel behind the buttons panel. Make sure you turn off AFT (Automatic Fine Tuning), then twiddle around to find the low end of the band. Easiest of all would be a really old set with a rotary dial, on which the frequencies will already be marked.

How it works

Lightning causes interference by generating a signal on and around 55 MHz. It's strong enough to completely light up the screen if closer than 10 miles or so.

GOOD FORECAST, BAD PICTURE

The high pressure that brings good weather has an odd effect on your analogue TV. When the picture goes squiffy the consolation for the urban bushman is that it can be explained with a neat bit of weather science.

If your picture is normally clear and you suddenly start to see evenly spaced stripes or bars across the screen in a 'Venetian blind' effect, then there's good weather on the way. That's all there is to it really. Try adjusting the aerial. If you can't fix it, the effect is definitely caused by high pressure. The picture won't improve till the weather worsens, which seems fair.

There isn't long left to view TV on an analogue signal, so make the most of this while you can. In our digital future it will become a distant memory. I already have my own nostalgic image stored away of a hot teenage summer trying to watch Borg and Connors battle it out over five sets through the stripey-green snow on the TV.

How it works

High pressure allows TV signals to reach areas they wouldn't normally get to, which can mean that your TV starts to pick up a new signal alongside the one it's already tuned to. This co-channel interference is what causes that familiar old Venetian blind effect.

THE TRUTH ABOUT THE ZAPPER

A visitor from Mars would know immediately that the TV zapper's important to us; why else would we give it such a variety of names and appear so bereft whenever it's out of our sight? It's our equivalent of the speaking stick that they pass around in mud huts when somebody wants to talk, except of course the zap is usually a sign to shut up. But it's an honour to hold it, a symbol of power and control. And here's a technique for keeping it in your grasp wherever you are in the house

Wherever we live, whatever our accent or upbringing, the name we give the zapper changes from house to house; it's a one-word micro-dialect specific to our home. Some terms are common (the clicker), some are rare (the wand), but hardly anyone uses the proper name (the remote control). Here are some I like: The onner-offer, the flipper, the doofer (or hoofer-doofer), the buttons, the (fat) controller, the trolls, the mote, and my mother's very own 'the psss-pssst'.

This technique for channel changing is especially recommended for snooker fans.

REMOTE CONTROL FREAK

The beam from the zapper is invisible to humans, and as a result the people you share your telly with prefer not to think about how it works, writing it off as a piece of magic. But really it's infrared light, which is light from a part of the spectrum we can't see, and because it's light it can bounce off mirrors (which shouldn't surprise anyone, but still does). This all makes for a good way to retain control over your living room.

Just configure a system of mirrors so you have a direct line of sight to the TV from the kitchen/dining room/study. Point the remote at the image of the TV and zap as normal. The rule is: if you can see it, you can zap it. It's especially handy if the kids are watching in one room and you're cooking fish fingers in another.

ZAPPER HOKUM

Like all important icons in our lives, the zapper is often the subject of half-truths and outright lies. One claim I've seen too much of recently is the suggestion that you can make an emergency replacement with a torch and a plastic lens. Don't believe it, no matter how convincing the website and video clip may appear. The remote works by sending a digital signature with encoded commands, far too complex to be copied by a flash of light from a torch. The zapper can do many things, but it's no bullshit detector; for that engage the brain.

CARPET STEALTH

Whether you're avoiding waking the children, avoiding detection after a night out or avoiding the in-laws, there are times when the ability to creep around the home without making a sound is a precious thing.

This is where you need your slippers. They are to you as the soft-soled moccasin was to the Seminole Indian, the expert trackers of the American woodland. By adapting the wisdom of the Seminole we turn creeping downstairs into an exercise in primitive stealth. Using his feet to feel the way, the noble hunter could creep across the forest floor in total silence, creating a picture of every twig and rock underfoot. If this is too hard with slippers try it with socks* and pick your path between the Lego bricks and those electronic toys ready to go off at the merest touch.

THE SIX GOLDEN RULES OF CARPET STALKING

1. SLIPPERS: Use them to feel the way.

2. HEEL FIRST: On carpet always bring the heel down first.

3. FEET STRAIGHT: On carpet, to avoid a giveaway 'rip' as your foot brushes against the pile of the carpet, it's vital that your feet are straight so that the big toe points the way.

4. EDGES: Avoid creaky floorboards by treading on edges near the wall, especially on staircases and bare floors.

* Slippers are quieter so what you lose in touch you may gain in stealth.

5. ATTIRE: Remove noisy clothing to avoid 'trouser swish'. Corduroy is a favoured fabric for hunters because it's relatively quiet.

6. SWITCH OFF: Don't fret, just believe you won't be heard. The leopard doesn't have self-doubt as it stalks its prey; nor should you.

To avoid squeaks when opening a door, dab some cooking oil on the hinge with a tissue. It does its work in seconds. To be doubly sure, apply upward pressure as you turn the handle.

A note on carpets: the shorter and tighter the weave, the noisier the carpet. Shag pile is preferred for stalking in slippers. On natural flooring, go for socks; never stalk in bare feet (unless powdered) in case they stick.

THE INDOOR FORAGER

Watching a TV survival expert eating bugs and berries in the wilderness can make you feel you're missing out. One solution would be to head for the Amazon to root around for edible leaves and medicinal shrubs. But don't bother; there's more than enough in the pot plants and vases around the house, and this way you can fit your foraging into an ad break. But do consult your flower guide first, to be certain you know which plants are definitely edible and which plants aren't.

HOUSE PLANTS AND FLOWERS — IDENTIFICATION GUIDE FOR THE INDOOR FORAGER

Over the page you'll find my guide to some common indoor edible plants. Always give them a good wash before eating and follow the guidelines closely. If you're in any doubt, don't eat it.

SPIDER PLANT

CHRYSANTHEMUM

SPIDER PLANT (LATIN NAME CHLOROPHYTUM)

Habitat: Usually found in hanging baskets or on top of speakers in a student bedsit.

Edible uses: All of the plant is safe to eat, and the tender plantlets that shoot off the main stem are especially good in a stir fry.

Medicinal use: In India it's commonly eaten as a leaf vegetable but the real interest is in the root, thought to have a medicinal use as a natural Viagra.

CHRYSANTHEMUM

Habitat: Supermarket flower buckets, funeral bouquets.

Edible uses: The flowers and seeds are edible and the leaves make a tasty tea. The variety called chop-suey greens (*Chrysanthemum coronarium spatiosum*) is especially good and rich in vitamins; eat young shoots cooked or raw, and leaves raw in a salad. The flower petals, blanched quickly in boiling water, are a decorative addition to salads.

ALOE VERA   **CHINESE LANTERN**   **MIXED BOUQUET**

ALOE VERA

Habitat: Designer flats, doctors' surgeries.

Medicinal use: A handy first-aid kit, especially good for soothing little burns, cuts and grazes. Just make a slit down a leaf, and rub the gel over the affected area. You can eat parts of some varieties, but it's a bit of a bother and strictly applies to only certain varieties, so best not to go there.

CHINESE LANTERN

Habitat: Auntie's sideboard.

Edible uses: If you've got a sweet tooth, these are for you. The flower is good raw or cooked, on its own or as part of a salad. The longer the flower is open, the sweeter it gets.

MIXED BOUQUETS

Habitat: Anywhere on Valentine's Day, Mother's Day.

Edible uses: Petals help any dish to cut a dash, so root around in a mixed bouquet for your favourites. Rose petals are especially palatable, a sprinkling of carnations makes a peppery addition to any meal, and tulips have a fresh taste, a bit like cucumber.

THE YUCCA – A ONE-STOP ACTIVITY CENTRE

It's one of the most common plants in the indoor environment. You've been watering it all these years; now it's time for some payback.

You can eat it, make rope and blankets with it, weave baskets and carve figurines, and it's the best wood bar none for lighting fires, so it's not surprising that Native American tribes mythologised the powers of the yucca. If you are prepared to sacrifice part of the root and trunk you have a day of yucca fun ahead, rounded off nicely with this evening's fire-lighting ceremony.

Which variety?

If you bought your yucca tree somewhere like Ikea there's a good chance its variety is the giant yucca (*Yucca elephantipes*) – which has all the qualities mentioned above. Most other yuccas do as well, but it's best to check. Another common variety is Spanish Bayonet (*Yucca aloifolia*), which is considered the best to eat.

Uses
YUCCA CHOPSTICKS

Time: one hour

The smooth wood is perfect to eat from, and splits easily. Start with a branch that looks about the right size to get one or two pairs of chopsticks from it and split it down the middle. Whittle away until one end of each is rounded, leaving the other end in its raw twig-like state for rustic authenticity.

YUCCA BRUSHES

Time: two hours

You need to have prepared for this by soaking some leaves in water for a couple of weeks. Now pound them with a stone to get rid of the green pulp until just the fibres are left. Tie a bunch of fibres close to one end. The Navajo would bind one end tight for use as a hair brush; the other, looser, end served as a clothes brush. Or, if you prefer, wind the fibres to make string, rope, baskets or a blanket (maybe just a very small one).

YUCCA FLOWER FRITTER

Time: 30 minutes

To do the least damage to your plant just eat the flower petals; they're good raw but best lightly cooked (dusted in flour and fried in oil for five minutes). If your yucca has a fruit you're in for a juicy treat. The stem of the flower is edible too, best peeled and boiled like asparagus. All to be eaten with the yucca chopsticks, of course.

YUCCA SOAP

Time: 40 minutes

Take a bit of the root and crush it in a bowl of water until it starts to go sudsy. The more you work at it, the more lather you get. Now you're ready for the Navajo hairwash, all the rage in the spas of New Mexico.

THE POWER-ASSISTED YUCCA FIRE-LIGHTING CEREMONY

In general, friction fire lighting by rubbing sticks is far too much bother. With some dried yucca, however, you have the best chance you're going to get of pulling it off, which has a certain satisfaction of its own. You can match the TV expert without leaving the living room.

It's all down to the yucca's uniquely low ignition temperature. To experience the thrill, without the sweat, here's what you'll need:

- dried yucca wood (after harvesting, leave for a week somewhere dry and warm)
- a power drill with blunt drill tip
- a ball of tinder; shredded paper/wool

Carve a small bowl-shaped dent into your yucca* and drill down into this until it begins to smoke. You need a blunt drill so that you don't bore through the soft wood too quickly.

Once the friction creates enough heat for the yucca wood to start smoking – you'll see it and smell it at the same time – keep going a little longer. Now whip the drill away and look for a tiny red-hot lump – or a'coal'. Very quickly, tip your coal into the tinder ball, blowing on it gently in the way you've seen on all those survival shows.

If you don't succeed at first keep trying. Or use a match.

Now put up a few shelves – you may as well, now that you've got the drill out.

THE CEILING SUNDIAL

The ceiling sundial brings the intrigue of the celestial cycle, of solstices and seasons, into your bedroom, and it's a pretty good way to tell if you're late for work as well.

Lying in bed one morning looking at the lines of sunlight thrown across

* The bowl is to help stop the drill from slipping.

the ceiling by reflections from the car windscreen below, I invented the ceiling sundial. I really did, even though Sir Isaac Newton had done the same, 350 years earlier. Whether it's the father of modern physics, you or me, it's pretty obvious that an ability to tell the time by looking at your bedroom ceiling is a thing worth having.

All you need is a mirror positioned on your window ledge so that a spot of light is thrown onto your ceiling. This is the simplest form of sundial; it needs the least equipment, it's fast to set up and, best of all, the space available on the ceiling allows for a bigger dial, giving extreme accuracy.

It only works if you have a south-facing bedroom, or at least a view of the southern sky from your room (anywhere between SW and SE facing is perfect).

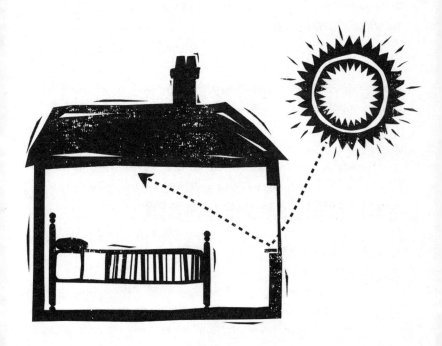

As well as a south-facing room and available ceiling you need:

- a small mirror
- glue or tape
- a pencil
- a clock.

FIXING THE MIRROR

In the morning, fix the mirror to the window sill (or a sash halfway up) so that it reflects a spot of light onto the ceiling. Position the mirror horizontally, as high (close to the ceiling) as you can get it.* Now follow the progress of the spot and mark its position every hour with a pencil.

Well done, you now have your very own spot dial, or at least the makings of one. The dial part (the equivalent of the clock face) takes a bit longer.

How it works

Before deciding how to mark your dial on the ceiling you need a basic grasp of how a sundial works. I'll cover it in three points.

1. Everything the sun does outside is the inverse of what happens on the ceiling. As it moves across from east to west the reflected beam moves across the ceiling west to east. The lower the sun in the sky, the further into your room the beam is projected.

2. The route of the spot changes daily, sweeping across the ceiling between two extremes: the winter and summer solstices. In the middle of these extremes is the equinox; that's the moment every 21 March and 22 September when the sun follows the same course in the sky and the days are exactly the same length as the nights. Mark out your dial on a date that's as close to the equinox as possible; this will help you position the equinox line (the mid point of your dial) close to the middle of the ceiling.

3. The hours fall within flared bands that radiate from a centre point somewhere outside your window.

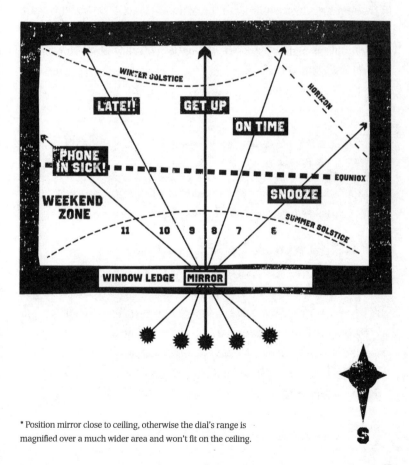

* Position mirror close to ceiling, otherwise the dial's range is magnified over a much wider area and won't fit on the ceiling.

THE DIAL

Now you're ready to mark your dial. Start the whole process in the morning, close to the time you want the dial to be most effective.

Look at the time and position the mirror so that it throws a spot on the ceiling wherever you think best, remembering that you need to be able to see the time easily when lying in bed. Leave space for the hours you'd like to come before and after.

Diehard sundial fans mark a central 'meridian' – the line the sun crosses at midday. But that's way too late. I prefer to make 9 o'clock the centre of things – one side is a lie-in, the other side isn't. By restricting the range to the vital few hours of the morning your dial can be more accurate, and you don't need such a big ceiling.

Seventeenth-century sundial obsessives started young. Isaac Newton drew his first ceiling sundial as a boy of 12. And at just 16 the young Christopher Wren drew an elaborate dial on the ceiling of his room at Oxford. Wren's sundial came a few years before Newton's, who was 5 at the time.

THE OFFICIAL LINE OF LATENESS

Mark the hours with stickers or pencil crosses (you still need your clock at this point). Before you begin to mark in your hour lines you need some of the year to pass. Mark the same time at the equinox and one of the solstices (or any two days a few months apart) and draw straight lines between them. Once you've got these hour lines in place, the dial starts to take shape. I use masking tape first before committing to paint, allowing me to tweak the lines later for supreme accuracy.

I'd start by marking only the hour by which you have to be out of bed making the simplest, clearest dial of all: a new meridian – the official line of lateness.

THE BEDROOM SHRINE

Five thousand years ago the inhabitants of Orkney built Maes Howe, a stone chamber expertly aligned so that on the winter solstice the setting sun sends a shaft of light along the entry passage to hit the back wall where the bones of the ancient elders were buried. Going to see it is a pretty good way to enthuse children with the whole idea of the celestial calendar. Or you could just show them the Indiana Jones movie that uses the same idea. Either way, you need to know that you can adapt the window-sill mirror trick to make your own bedroom version of this sacred shrine.

- Pick your significant date (say a birthday).
- Through careful positioning of the mirror mark a suitable spot where the celestial beam will hit the wall.
- Now position your chosen icon (football poster, cartoon character, darts trophy) so that at sunrise or sunset on the given day it is kissed by the golden rays that peep over the horizon. You will need to provide the soundtrack yourself.

Alternative suggestion: I often use the sunspot as a random CD-selection technique. But as a seasonal touch you could arrange things so that at 10am on 25 December a sunbeam illuminates the Phil Spector Christmas CD on the shelf, in preparation for its annual outing.

Urban bushcraft through the ages: Benjamin Thompson (Count Rumford) 1753–1814

To round off our exploration of the indoors, here's an account of what happens when a great inventor turns his mind to the home.

Benjamin Thompson was by all accounts a scoundrel, and a good-looking one too. One biographer says he was 'overbearingly arrogant and had no friends', which seems a bit pointed. Anyway, he had to leave his native America in a hurry after he backed the wrong side in the War of Independence and spent the rest of his life in Europe, picking up wives and titles while pursuing his career as a scientist.

But what I love about him is that his boundless curiosity was unfettered by the snobbish view that science is too grand to be turned to domestic matters. A lover of the mundane, he begged to differ with this supercilious assumption. 'It is really astonishing how little attention is paid to things near us, and which are familiar to us ... How few persons are there who ever took the trouble to bestow a thought on the subject in question, though it is, in the highest degree, curious and interesting!', he wrote.

Rumford's area of expertise was heat, and everything associated with it. But there were no steam locomotives and spinning machines for him. Instead, he revolutionised the domestic fireplace forever, did the same for the cooker and then repeated the feat for the coffee percolator. And then came his *chef-d'œuvre*. While remarking upon the low heat conductivity of egg white he found another of his fantastic domestic applications for science when he gave the world Baked Alaska.* I can't imagine that Leonardo, for all his much-vaunted inventiveness, would have thought to put ice cream inside a baked dessert.

---

* The only blemish on Rumford's record is that he didn't call it Baked Alaska, but Omelette Surprise.

THE SIOUX ALARM CLOCK

At times when you don't want to trust your fate to a gadget powered by a couple of AAs, remember the Sioux warrior.

When a Sioux needed to wake early to go into battle or to follow a trail he simply used his bladder as an early morning call. The earlier he wanted to be woken, the more water he drank at bedtime. I've tried it once and the calibration needed some improvement, but the technique can't be faulted.

2.
TRAVEL WITH A
SMALL 'T'

'So, which way did you come; was it M5 – M6 – M62?'
'Yes, that's right. I was going to go M5 – M42 – M1,
but there was a contra-flow at Solihull.'
'Ah, right.'

I don't think I've ever arrived at the end of a long drive and not found myself part of this little men-only ritual: the route conversation. I've been a keen student of this one for a few years, and I marvel at the variety of ways we can find to tee up a bout of swapping road numbers. Both men are reciting a script they know by heart, slotting the pieces into a puzzle that celebrates an obsession with how we got here. I always want to go for a little high five at the end, but that hasn't quite caught on.

I mention this because it helps identify what this section is all about: travel with a small 't'. The urban bushman isn't interested in capital 'T' travel – with trips of a lifetime; he's focused on being home by teatime. He doesn't care about the opening times of the Genghis Khan memorial in Ulan Bator;

he wants to know how to get the best seat on the number 58 into town.

Travel doesn't have to have an exotic destination to broaden the mind. Simply bring the spirit of the great explorers to the daily commute turns it from lost time into a heroic endeavour. My favourite Victorian, Sir Francis Galton, wrote in *The Art of Travel:* 'Thescientific advantages of travel are enormous to a man prepared to profit by them.'* And it's in that spirit that e learn how to navigate by satellite dish or use a motorway trip to cook chicken wings on the car engine. Whatever our chosen mode of travel, we're moving on in the name of science and of adventure.

MAN'S SPECIALIST SUBJECT

Men love routes; route maps and route conversations are their bread and butter. So when an applicant to the TV quiz *Mastermind* suggested as his specialist subject 'Routes to Anywhere in Mainland Britain by Road from Letchworth' you just knew he was going to be unbeatable. I imagined him sitting in the famous black chair in driving gloves rattling off a litany of road numbers in tribute to the inherent brilliance of man. But the BBC's producers rejected his application. I think they were scared.

* As further encouragement to the prospective traveller he added this consoling thought: 'Savages rarely murder new-comers.'

CARS: BUSHMAN BEHIND THE WHEEL

I know that cars are useful and I do understand that they arouse in people deep passions, but let's not pretend that man and motor are made for each other. Don't get me wrong, the potential is tremendous, but the practicalities are a problem.

The car is a symbol of freedom, yet we spend about an hour a week trying to find a parking space. We dream about 0–60 in five seconds but most of the time we're outpaced by pedestrians. We love the privacy, but all we do in a traffic jam is pick our nose and adjust the mirrors.

The best way I can sum up our relationship with cars is this: man has the ingenuity and brilliance to invent the car and yet whenever he wants to go for a drive he can never find the bloody keys. And that's just frustrating. So it falls to the urban bushman to close some of the gaps that have opened up between men and motor cars and discover new ways for us and them to get along.

THE REAL HIGHWAY CODE

Humans evolved over thousands of years, while cars have been around for just a few decades. It's clear when you think about it that the person in the driving seat is a man first and a motorist second. This is the simple secret behind the vocabulary of signs and signals that are the real Highway Code.

All mechanical means to communicate with another driver are flawed. A flash of headlights meant as a friendly invitation to pull over can be seen as a hostile shot across the bows, and the horn is just as bad. We have no evolutionary experience with cars, and so we end up judging them on completely flawed criteria, seeing them as if they were people, finding an angry expression in the headlights or a nasty word in a perfectly innocent number plate.

The key is simply this: forget the car and make contact with the driver. In anonymous isolation behind the wheel, he's free to assert his baser instincts and probably will. But adding a social dimension (however fleeting) changes all that for good. This explains why drivers with the roof down are much less likely to misbehave – we can see them.

The ultimate deterrent to aggressive driving is eye contact. Cyclists and pedestrians instinctively know how to use the human eye as the ultimate traffic signal and they do it all the time. Once they make eye contact they know that the driver's seen them. But that's not all. Eye contact has a deep primal meaning. It's a signal that we're no longer dealing with a ton of metal moving at speed, but another human, and that changes the rules considerably.

Eye contact

The change in our behaviour when you take away eye contact shows its deep significance. It's so important that we've developed an almost supernatural ability; when somebody looks us in the eye, even at a distance, in an instance, we *know*. There are a few things that stop this from happening: dark glasses, motorbike visors, and most significantly of all, travelling at over 20mph.

DRIVING BY NUMBERS

How to tell where you are by road numbers

We all know a lot of roads by their number, and they normally start with M or with A. Most people have spotted also that there's a kind of logic to it, with the A1 and M1 doing a similar job and all roads that have 2 as their first number being down in the southeast corner of England. But once the whole system is revealed, you'll never look at another road number the same way again.*

---

* The information that follows is fascinating, I accept. But take it easy, and if you start to visit the specialist road-numbering websites that are out there, maybe you should seek help.

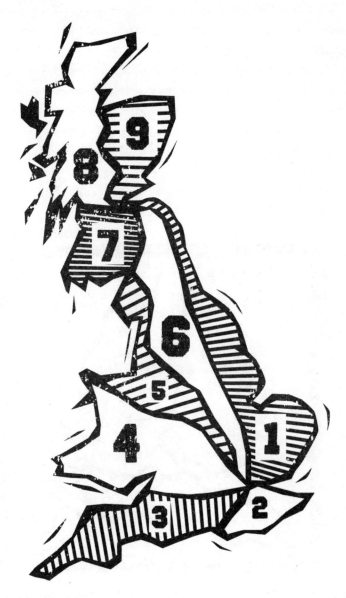

Britain's road zones

Our roads are numbered under a system that seemed like a good idea in 1923. Motorways and A roads are numbered by the same rules but on a different system. I hope you're keeping up so far.

It starts simply enough. Mainland Britain is divided into numbered 'sectors' or zones. Each zone is bordered by a major road and/or the coastline. Any road that starts in that zone takes the number of the zone as the first digit of its name.

The main routes 1–6 radiate outwards from London, and 7–9 from Edinburgh.

There are exceptions of course, as with any rule. But it's fairly consistent; for example Zone 3 is where the A30, the A38 and the B3088 all start.

The motorway zones of England and Wales

MOTORWAYS

Motorways don't use the same zones. Scotland has a system of its own, but it's England and Wales where it's most complicated, so let's deal with that first.

The system works like the A roads, with any motorway that starts in one of the specified zones taking that number as its first digit . . . hence M61, M62, M66 etc. The M25 starts just south of the Dartford Tunnel in Kent, in zone 2.

It gets confusing with zones 4 and 5. Because the M5 runs from Birmingham, not London, it borders the wrong side of zone 5, and there's another numbering nightmare where the M4 and M5 cross near Bristol. All this can be hard to take in at first, but after time these peculiar wrinkles in the system just add an additional layer of interest, and make great fodder for dropping into your next route conversation.

Where possible, the motorway numbers mimic the A and B road numbers, but not always. And don't look for logic or chronology in the way the A and B road numbers are allocated. You won't find any.

SCOTLAND

Scotland's system is blissfully simple. Motorways were built to relieve existing routes, and took the same number as those A-routes. On the downside this means that Scotland has an M876, simply because it follows the route of the A876.

Urban bushcraft through the ages:
Sir Francis Galton

Here's a bit of spiritual uplift from a pioneer of our craft, a man who inspires the urban bushman to shake off conventional wisdom and to see everyday life with the eye of an explorer making landfall on a new continent.

Sir Francis Galton was a great Victorian writer and explorer who saw travel as an art and a science, and felt it was his job to further them both, which he does in his masterpiece, *The Art of Travel*. For Sir Francis, exploration wasn't about having the right kit and looking good in a bandanna; it was the noble endeavour of a civilised mind.

When travelling in Africa he took with him theodolites, writing desks and ink stands. He always packed a dinner jacket, insistent the dress code wouldn't slip just because he was in the tropics. His version of the gap-year traveller's money belt involved secreting gemstones under the flesh, allowing the skin to seal it in 'as it would over a bullet'. But the thing I like best of all is his dedication to the art of rolling up sleeves.

Like all of us when we roll up our sleeves Sir Francis knew that there was every chance that it would be just a minute or two before they'd roll back down again – which is inconvenient when sewing gemstones into one's own arm. Plainly Sir Francis was not the sort to tolerate this kind of let-down. Instead, he determined to fix sleeve-rolling for good, so he started to rethink the whole procedure. After some experimentation he made a breakthrough with some Victorian blue-sky thinking that's a gift to us all from the great age of exploration and discovery.

> When you have occasion to tuck up your shirt sleeves, recollect that the way of doing so is not to begin by turning the cuffs inside out, but outside in. The sleeves must be rolled up inwards towards the arm and not the reverse way. In the one case the sleeves will remain tucked up for hours; in the other they become loose every five minutes. (Francis Galton, *The Art of Travel*, 1855)

Sir Francis's book gives sleeve-rolling as much space as all that really obvious explorer stuff (you know the sort of thing; how to cross a river with a mule, the correct way to approach a native). For him, fixing the small stuff improves your life as much as the big macho set pieces. Quite right, Sir.

GALTON'S CODE FOR ADVENTURE

I really like Sir Francis. This man would never compromise, and there's a lot to learn from his approach. In fact I've distilled the essence of his outlook for the bullet-point generation. After all, no urban adventurer is fully equipped before they're acquainted with Galton's Code.

- Nothing is too trivial for reinvention by the adventurer.
- Maintain standards of dress at all times.
- Use tools you can trust; shun new-fangled gadgets.
- It's what you find out that matters, not how flashy your kit is.

FINDING PARKED CARS THE NATIVE AMERICAN WAY

Every evening millions of us park our cars on the street where we live. No wonder then it's so hard to find a space out there, and we have to drive miles to get a spot. The end result is that we wake up every morning and wonder where the hell we left the car last night. The standard response to the problem is to defend your parking space with a scaffolding plank across two chairs. But for urban bushman it's a chance to hone a craft borrowed from the great native tribes of North America. And it's less likely to provoke a war with the neighbours.

It depends on learning a system of 'blazes'. These are the secret trail signs Native Americans used to show others the way – blazing the trail. In this adaptation for the urban reservation the trail leads discreetly to your parked car. If you pass this on to friends and family you can share the location of the car day or night. There's no need to ask where it is, just follow the blazes.

Blazes are useful whenever parking in a large car park or parking on the street every day for work. For lazier days another popular method is to take a picture of the car (and car park row number) on your camera phone.

Playing at cowboys and Indians used to brief a boy in the ways of the wild. You learned how to shoot a Winchester rifle and rope steers, how to holler like an Apache brave and use bird sounds as a secret language. And all long before you'd even seen a Clint Eastwood movie. But those days rode off into the sunset long ago. The turning point came in 1977. The holiday movie of the summer took the plot of a John Wayne Western called *The Searchers* and transplanted it into another world that would inspire the games of a new generation of young romantics. The film was *Star Wars*. This all explains why kids now don't know, by putting their ear to the ground, how many riders are approaching. But they're pretty good at Jedi mind games.

MAKING BLAZES

There are a couple of choices. You can use chalk or some kind of marker (such as tape) to record your trail, or make blazes out of stuff lying around like gravel, grass, litter or twigs. This organic approach is more satisfying. But the benefit of using chalk or tape is that it's far easier to spot (for the initiated) and can be especially useful when laying a trail for somebody else to follow.

Native American blazes conformed to a simple grammar; you just need to adapt them for your native landscape, using bits of urban detritus.

With found items:

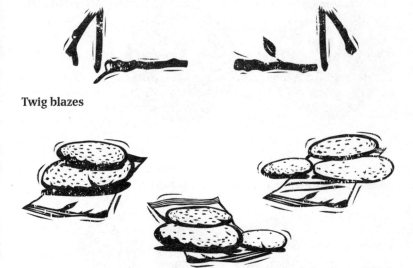

Twig blazes

Rock blazes: a crisp packet or scrap of litter under the bottom rock helps the blaze to stand out.

Marked blazes

Marked on street signs, road signs or each street corner, these blazes create your own coded directions, legible to the initiated only. It's graffiti's grown-up brother.

The circle means TRAIL; the line shows which way to go, LEFT or RIGHT; no line means straight on.

Once you've mastered this you can get a bit more communicative:

KEEP GOING, NEXT RIGHT and KEEP GOING, NEXT LEFT

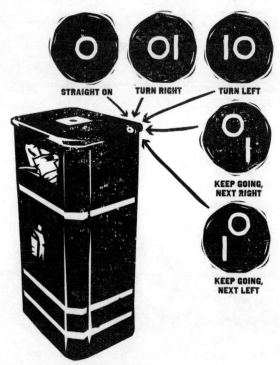

Bon blazes: graffiti's grown-up brother

WHY MEN LOVE GIVING DIRECTIONS

There can't be many things that the human male enjoys giving away to total strangers, but offering directions is one of them. We all know the sense of swelling pride when someone asks you to direct them: it's so strong that when you see a person poring over a street map you even get an urge to offer to help. Anyone who really needs assistance – struggling with a heavy suitcase, for example, or with small children – can forget it, but when it comes to directions we love to show we know.

Conversely, we hate asking for directions; it's a sign of weakness, showing that we don't know. Being given directions is so repellent that it's almost impossible to listen. We've all done it, and we've all seen it happen. You're giving out directions and you can see by the look in their eyes that it's just not sinking in. They were with you up to the second piece of information (turn left just after the Texaco garage . . . or was it just before?). But from then on, forget it. They're nodding politely but, inside, they've got their fingers in their ears while shouting 'not listening, not listening!' They just can't help it.

BLAZE THE TRAIL TO YOUR HOUSE

Instead of rubbing up against the male ego in a rather unpleasant way, share a primeval tracking opportunity next time you need to direct a visitor to your house. By laying a few simple blaze trails from the big obvious start points you can challenge anyone to spot the trail to your door. It's a test of your carefully laid blazes, the person in question gets to use their instinct for a trail, and nobody has to listen to any instructions; a win-win situation.

CAR-ENGINE COOKERY

DON'T SAY 'ARE WE THERE YET?'
JUST ASK 'IS IT DONE YET?'

Using the heat of your engine to cook while you drive is a classic of improvisational brilliance, adding value to every gallon of fuel by delivering a piping hot meal on arrival at your chosen destination. But economics and convenience are only the start of under-the-bonnet cuisine's attraction. It's an extension of our love affair with the car itself; it represents a man's freedom and is something he can get completely obsessive about.

The principle of wrapping your food in foil and sticking it on a hot engine is simple, and many a good meal's been had by putting a hotdog somewhere snug under the bonnet, clocking up 40 miles or so, and tucking in. But that's the equivalent of a boy scout chucking a foil-wrapped potato into a bonfire. The joy is in the refining: each foray sharpens the appreciation of the special relationship between the three variables; journey time, mileage and choice of dish.

Instead of oven temperature and cooking time, recipes give mileage and speed. For instance, at 65mph prawns cook in about 50 miles, chicken wings need about 130 miles and a full roast dinner is done in 300 miles.

The relationship between the three variables in engine cookery is echoed in several car makers' logos. The three-pronged star of the Mercedes symbol is an especially handy reminder.

50-MILE HOT DOG

There's a lot to learn before you can safely cook a proper meal on your engine, but experience is a great teacher. Next time you're due to take a 50- or 60-mile drive, turn it into a field trip and launch your career as a car-engine chef.

Wrap a couple of hot dog sausages or frankfurters in foil (tightly) and find somewhere to wedge or jam them snugly on top of the engine. Keep them away from moving parts and make sure they're held in position when the bonnet's down.

Pack a couple of buns (plus ketchup/mustard) and some oven gloves (they're what the glove compartment is really for), and set off. On arrival, check out the hot dogs for heat; if hot, tuck in and enjoy your first car-cooked meal. If the hot dogs are still cool, put it down to experience, and read on.

CAR COOKERY KIT

- Oven gloves
- Tongs (for access to especially tight spots)
- Hot dogs
- Mustard/relish
- Herbs/spices
- Spare foil
- Notebook for recipes and observations

WHEN TO COOK WITH THE CAR

- *Camping trips*: You've arrived, it's raining and you've got to put the tent up. Thank heavens for piping hot burgers and crispy oven chips.
- *Dinner party (guest)*: Offer to turn up with something hot to bring straight to the table – a guaranteed talking point.
- *Dinner party (host)*: Assign each guest to bring a different course, based on how far they have to travel.
- *Fishing trips*: Enjoy the catch of the day at its freshest, after a twenty-minute drive to a secluded picnic spot.

GETTING STARTED – THE TWO TESTS

The cardinal rule of engine-block* cookery is to work with the 'configuration' of your car; its individual engine anatomy. Two basic tests can help you look at what's beneath the bonnet with the eye of the chef** to discover the best parts for quick cooking (hottest), for slower cooking (coolest), and the shape and size of all the nooks and crannies where you can slot in some food.

Test 1: The heat test

Time: ten minutes

Take your car for a five-minute drive to get it warm, park and lift the bonnet. Hover your hand over various parts of the engine to see how hot they are. Be extremely careful, as the aim is to feel the heat WITHOUT getting burned.

If you wish, you can integrate this test with the 50-mile hot dog (see page 67), and use your spare hot dog as a thermometer. If it sizzles, you've hit somewhere hot.

Remember that you're looking for a range of spots with different temperatures so that you'll be able to cook two very different dishes at the same time. Ignore plastic parts – they won't get hot.

Usually, the hottest part of the engine will be the exhaust manifold (the big iron tube running the length of the engine from front to back with two, four or six other tubes from the engine joining it) . On older cars, the top of the engine block can be a good place too. As you go, keep an eye out for any likely crevices or crannies where you could fit a foil-wrapped parcel of food. If you have a natural dip or indentation on top of the engine block, and it's hot, you're off to a good start.

---

* The engine block is the main chunk of the engine in the middle. It has fuel injectors and spark plugs (with cables attached) sticking into it. This is where the power and heat come from.
** Expert car-engine cooks take pride in having different recipes for different cars, which gives an idea of how different each car can be.

Test 2: The foil crunch test

Time: ten minutes

Now that you have an idea of where you might be able to cook on the engine, you need to find out what you can fit into it, and where.

Make a loose ball of foil and put it on any likely spots on top of the engine. Through trial and error find the clearance of the space by seeing how much the ball is crushed when you close the bonnet. Be precise, so that the bonnet will hold food parcels snugly in position.

Use the same principle to find out the size of each of the cooking cavities. Now when you cook you'll know where each item will fit best. Bulk up smaller items to the right size with extra foil.

ENGINE ENVY

Now that you're paying attention to what's beneath the bonnet, everyone's car can become a source of interest. The next time someone lifts the bonnet on their flashy V8 engine, have a look and drool, not at the thought of the power it generates but at the delights that could be so effortlessly cooked in that deep V-shaped indentation along the top of the engine block.

The Jaguar E-type is considered the prime example of this unique feature of the V8, and chefs have been known to fit enough fillet steak or rib-eye to cater for six persons with ease.

THE HIGHWAY COOKERY CODE

- Cook anything you'd cook in the oven, but avoid sloppy casseroles and stews (vibrations will spill juice everywhere).
- Triple wrap everything you cook in foil.
- Fit your food to the spaces available, overwrap to fill the space.
- Safety first! Only put food in and take it out with the engine off.

- Never place food near the line that joins the accelerator pedal to the engine or any of the air intakes.
- Don't pull any wires or force a package to fit where it's too big.
- Always use tongs or oven gloves to remove hot food.

THE CAR-B-Q

Cooking on the move has a rich heritage that connects medieval horsemen of Asia with American truckers of the 1950s. For both, it was a ritual that defined their nomadic way of life; one lot put raw steak under their saddle to give it a pounding in preparation for a victory feast,* the others heated hot dogs on their exhaust manifold to provide a lazy lay-by snack.

The car-b-q recaptures that spirit of romantic adventure. It's food designed to be eaten out of doors. As the smell of your mixed kebabs and steak wafts through the grille, you can catch the eye of the driver in the outside lane knowing that you're the real king of the road around here.

1. Plan your journey time and select your meat and fish course to suit (see cooking guidelines below).
2. Follow pre-cooking or marinade directions from any conventional recipe. Think about catering for the ravenous nomad inside you. Which will it be: the Mongolian horseman or the American lorry driver?
3. Wrap the food in a variety of packet sizes to fit the available slots and secure them in place.
4. Unwrap it and serve.

---

* The horsemen in question were the Tartar warriors of Siberia, hence Steak Tartare.

To spice it up why not add a few side dishes like stuffed peppers, flat breads or sliced aubergine to accompany your meat, fitting them in where you can. Vegetable dishes can go into the cooler spots of the engine.

ROUGH COOKING TIMES AT AVERAGE SPEED OF 55MPH		
ALWAYS ENSURE THE SPECIFIC FOOD HAS COOKED THROUGH PROPERLY		
Prawns	30–50 miles	up to 80 miles in cooler position
Fish	60 miles	up to 100 miles in cooler position
Chicken wings	60–100 miles	up to 200 miles in cooler position
Chicken breasts	140–200 miles	up to 300 miles in cooler position
Baked potato	200 miles	up to 300 miles in cooler position
Diced spicy lamb	200 miles	up to 300 miles in cooler position

HARMFUL FUMES

A well-maintained engine won't emit foul or harmful by-products; they're all channelled into the exhaust. If you can smell your food cooking that's good news, because it means you'd also smell any nasty gases coming off your engine. If you can smell something nasty you need to get it checked urgently, whether you're cooking or not.

What's That Smell?

One last word of warning, in the form of a confession.

Last summer, my family began to comment on a dreadful smell in or around our car. I thought it would go and they'd soon stop fussing. But it didn't. Then a week or so later the terrible truth dawned on me. It was coming from under the engine, near the manifold. It could only be one thing – a lost piece of jerk chicken from a cooking foray at least a month earlier. Removing it was a hour-long operation (in the end I had to use an extendable umbrella handle). And it took a couple of days to get the smell out of my nose, and longer to get over the dented pride that came with such a schoolboy mistake. This is the first time my beloved family will learn the truth (if they read this far). The lesson from all this is to be strictly organised with all food placed on your engine. Leave nothing behind – count them out, and count them back.

BACKSEAT CHEFS

All the campfire classics for kids will work well on a car engine. The foil-wrapped banana (unpeeled) with chocolate stuffed inside through small slits in the skin is, of course, a classic. In a hot engine allow 30 miles to achieve gooey bliss. Baked apples need about 50 miles.

Chris Maynard and Bill Scheller introduced the world to gourmet engine cuisine in the 1980s with their book *Manifold Destiny*, which includes recipes such as Hyundai Halibut with Fennel, Poached Fish Pontiac and Cruise Control Tenderloin.

BANGERS FOR YOUR BANGER

Having just roasted some venison steak beneath the bonnet of my battered and mud-splattered BMW diesel estate (120 miles, still nice and pink inside), I realised the benefit of matching the car to the meat. Get it right and it just completes the picture.

Mini Cooper	Spicy chicken wings
Ford Mondeo	Burger, oven chips
Cortina Mk II	Gammon steak with pineapple
Land Rover	Trout with wild herbs
Porsche	Rib-eye steak
Vauxhall Corsa	Supermarket bangers

NEED A BOTTLE OPENER?

Most car-door mechanisms have a handy built-in bottle opener on the door frame. Look for the D-shaped loop of metal that keeps the door shut.

WINDSCREEN BAKERY

This is great for keeping kids amused on a camping trip. You use the car but you don't even have to turn it on, just make sure it's in the sun. Mix some biscuit dough or flapjacks mix and put on a baking tray, then leave exposed to the sun inside a closed car for 2–3 hours and return to pick them up in time for afternoon tea.

On a sunny day, when temperatures can reach 30°C, a car's dashboard can heat up to around 90°C, which is perfect for baking biscuits.

THE BUSHMAN AT THE BUS STOP/COMMUTING

Cavemen commuted too; it's something we've always needed to do. And with ten thousand years or so of experience, we should be able to negotiate it without breaking into a sweat. By drawing on the wisdom of the great commuters of the past, the urban bushman takes the angst out of the daily trip to work and turns it into a twice-daily mini-holiday.

TWO STEPS TO A CALM COMMUTE
Step 1: The 60-minute rule

An hour of travel a day feels civilised. With two half-hour journeys, the brain has time to acclimatise and to assimilate. But it's more than just a feeling that tells us this is right; it's a commuting instinct that's as deeply pre-programmed into our primitive brain as the need for a good night's sleep.

Man is a territorial animal and likes to patrol his patch. The bigger the patch the better; that way we get more food, more mates, more of everything. But we're a cave animal as well, and so we want to finish our day curled up in the familiar fug of the family home. Now you see how commuting was born.

Physicist Cesare Marchetti was intrigued to know more and pulled together a load of research to show how long people spend each day in routine travel, whether from an African village or a Japanese city. He found it was all stunningly uniform; in all societies there's a tendency to organise our life so that a total of 1.1 hours a day is spent in transit.

Then he went on to show that this figure, 'Marchetti's Constant', hasn't changed throughout history. As evidence, he found that the size of Greek villages and ancient cities like Rome, Marrakesh and Persepolis, and even his native Venice, are all of a size that you can walk from the outskirts so the distance to the outskirts grew; to the centre in about half an hour. And as transport developed a half-hour by horse and cart, or Austin 7, each development pushing back the city limits.

Marchetti showed that 90 per cent of our total travel time is spent inside this 30-minute zone, and we have every reason to think it's always been that way. So if your commute is feeling more stressful than it should, recalibrate.

If it's under an hour there and back, stretch it out. And if it's running over, consider drastic action to hit the target time. Man has favoured a 30-minute each-way commute throughout his history, and that's some serious conditioning. You'd be a fool to fight it.

Step 2: The commute as a holiday

The *Star Trek* 'teleporter' always seemed like a good idea, getting beamed to wherever you want to be in a second. But hang on a minute; look at what you'd miss out on.

Travelling puts you in a bubble, protected from outside annoyance and irritations. The French philosopher Michel de Certeau called journeys like this an 'incarceration-vacation' and I know what he meant. You're captive, all you can do is sit there – and that's a huge relief.

Next time you're on a regular journey by bus or by train allow yourself to revel in the serene isolation. Look out of the window, switch off, and ask if life could be any better. Even the phone can't break the spell: reception is in and out, and you can hardly discuss the new marketing strategy in front of the whole carriage. Commuting is a holiday from the mania for productivity that fills the rest of your life. It's 'me-time', and it comes free with your ticket.

BUS SEATS AND HOW TO GET THEM

If the urban bushman is a sniper picking off the problems of daily life, then the daily struggle for a seat on a rush-hour bus or tube makes perfect target practice. As you line it up in the cross-hairs, go through your mental checklist . . .

- Is it part of your daily routine? Check!
- Is it stressing you out? Check!!
- Can we find a strategy to overcome it that's deeply satisfying? Check!!!

- Its fate is sealed: time for this nasty little threat to be neutralised.

If you follow the plan, put in the preparation and the planning, and leave nothing to chance; this is a mission that can be accomplished in under a week. Pep talk over; let's get on with it.

Operation 'Best Seat'
PHASE ONE: OBSERVATION

Look at your fellow passengers and notice the dead eyes and blank expressions. Notice the determination to push, shove and do whatever it takes to get themselves a seat or enough space to open the paper. They're just very bored; the whole thing's been stripped of manners and morals by the corrosive monotony of commuting. Rather than face the crushing tedium as civilised humans, they've switched off and handed the controls to the caveman brain. And for our purposes, this couldn't be better, because bored cavemen are entirely predictable, which makes it easy for the urban bushman to gain the critical edge, and more importantly, get a seat.

Exercise: Pick three or four travellers at random. Imagine them as hairy savages in bare feet and leopard-print all-in-ones, as they eye each other from beneath prominent brows, and fiddle with their flint axe-heads and iPhones. Retain this image as a constant reminder of whom you're really dealing with here.

PHASE TWO: SURVEILLANCE

Now look at yourself (to help, you may be able to catch a reflection of yourself in the window). Notice how you behave when you're settling in for several stops and when you're about to get off. What are the giveaway signs and micro-signals that reveal your travel plans? You'll start to spot the same things in other passengers. Keeping a backpack on, constantly looking around, shuffling the feet and zipping up the bag are all signs that you'll be moving soon; taking off a coat or settling into a book without looking up at the stops is a sure sign you're going long haul.

Exercise: Challenge yourself and a travel companion to nominate which passenger from a pre-selected pool of ten will be getting off next. If you get over 50 per cent you've graduated.

PHASE THREE: PICK YOUR TARGET

Start by studying the seat layout. Identify the best seats and the best spaces; i.e. those where you're likely to be most comfortable and have the best chance of getting a seat. You'll begin to realise that there's a hierarchy of seats and standing spaces.

Exercise: Look at the case study on p. 84 below, and draw up a plan for your regular bus or train carriage, with the seats numbered in order of preference. Do the same with the standing spaces. You won't need to think too hard about which seats/spaces are the best; you'll know in your gut. Now you have a plan on paper, you can devise a strategy to target the best seats.

The hierarchy of seats on the Tube: a case history

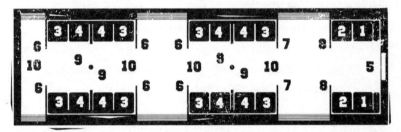

This diagram shows all tactically valid spots on a moderately full Tube carriage, ranked 1–10. Any unmarked positions are to be avoided.

SEATED

- *Position 1*: This is the top spot. You have only one neighbour, and the chance of a breeze from the door at the end of the carriage.
- *Position 2*: Also good, though beware of the person squashed against the glass screen (8). Both 1 and 2 are subjected to less passing traffic than other seats.
- *Position 3*: Less secluded than 2, but still good (only one neighbour).

- *Position 4*: The worst seat (two neighbours, minimal elbow room).

STANDING

- *Position 5*: Comfortable for leaning, with a vantage point over 1 and 2 if they become free, plus fresh air from the door at the end. Nobody can contest this spot, it's yours.
- *Positions 6–8*: Good leaning support and access to a number of seats.
- *Position 9*: No leaning support and only the central pole to hold on to, but a good chance to beat 6 or 7 to a vacated seat.
- *Position 10*: Skilful use of the body to block here can shield seat 3 until it's available to grab.

BATTLE ON THE CENTRAL LINE

As an out-of-towner I'm struck by the accomplished and instinctive performance of London's seasoned commuters. They sense a breeze in the tunnel and run for their train, they duck down No Entry passages, emerge at the escalator, and sweep through ticket barriers without breaking stride. So it's no surprise that seat hierarchy is ingrained in Tube culture, as I witnessed on a very crowded Central Line train at 5pm, the peak of the squeeze.

It began at a station when a newcomer stepped into position B (see diagram) on a crowded carriage. She had a bad spot near the door and made a bold opening gambit to take position A, one of the best standing positions on the carriage. She moved forward trying to shove the woman already at A further into the carriage. If she was lucky her victim wouldn't know the value of her spot.

But this was an experienced commuter, so she countered, pushing the newcomer back against the door. The newcomer shoved back again, but as

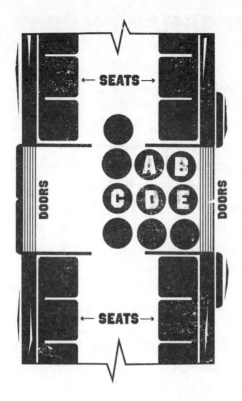

she did so a man in the inferior position E made a half-step towards position B. If successful this would force the newcomer into D, the worst spot of all (nothing to hold on to except other passengers, surrounded on all sides). So she retreated to defend her spot at B.

Suddenly A saw a seat and grabbed it in an instant (this is the great benefit of her position). D had been alert, anticipated the move, and slotted into position behind A in the seamless way only Tube commuters can. As for that poor woman at B I don't think she even noticed.

It was a dance performed in silence, with blank faces and dead eyes. And every day the Tube provides drama like this, for anyone tuned in enough to see.

THE BUSHMAN ON FOOT

In traditional bushcraft, the smelly damp sort that goes on in the woods, finding your way around the place on foot is a core skill. You can use a compass of course, but it's nicer to be able to manage without. So you have to look for the clues in nature that reliably point out north (or south, east or west). For instance, in Britain all windswept trees bend towards the east (because the prevailing wind is westerly), and moss prefers the damper north side of trees. Simple really.

The same kind of thing goes on in our urban environment, where there are modern equivalents of these aids to the wandering bushman. It's just that these techniques haven't made it into quite so many manuals and handbooks.

All this stuff is especially good when you're out and about. After all, you don't really need it at home. You already know which way your house faces thanks to your estate agent's fixation with whether or not your garden's 'south-facing'.

DIRECTION FINDING BY SKY DISH

Navigators of old used the stars to steer a course. Wherever you were on the globe you could look to the heavens and get a fix on your position. But in the modern 24-hour city most stars are blotted out. Thanks to light pollution, any form of navigation by astral means is completely out. Or is it? Here's a technique that's every bit as cosmic, and it works day or night.

The TV satellite dish is a convenient and reliable indicator of direction. And wherever you may wander in town, you're sure to spot one.

All you need to know is that Sky dishes all point at a spot just above the horizon in the southern sky 29 degrees east of due south. That's one third of the way round from south towards east on the compass. If you imagine the compass as a clock face, it's around the number five.

So once you've found which way the dish is facing, look at it as 5 o'clock. Then, just trace an imaginary line from the centre of the dish through where

6 o'clock would be. And that's south. I'll leave you to deduce north from there on your own (see illustration on p.87).

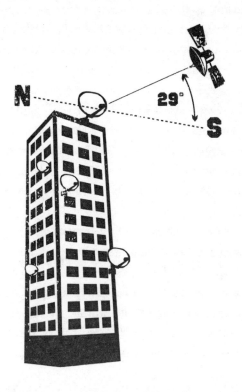

How it works

All TV satellites are in geostationary orbit. That means they hang above the equator beaming down on us from the same spot. It's all so that our tiny little dishes can pick them out. And in the UK the news for urban navigators is even better. Sky TV has a near monopoly on beaming game shows and suchlike to the UK from outer space. So all our dishes point to the same little cluster of satellites. And as every Sky dish installer in the country knows, that's 29 degrees E of S.

As you'll have realised already, there's another useful piece of information here. Because TV satellites are low in the sky, you can get a quick fix on north or south, wherever you are in the world. In the northern hemisphere (Europe, the USA, the Faroes etc.) all TV satellite dishes turn to the southern sky. In the southern hemisphere, which includes Australia (take note Rupert Murdoch), they're looking north.

THE BUSHMAN IN NEW YORK

In New York, streets are laid out on a grid. They say the avenues run north and the streets go east to west. They don't. In fact the whole thing is skewed by 29 degrees off true north. So what seems like north is more like north-northeast. Of course the streets that run across the grid are similarly squiffy.

With practical considerations at heart, map-makers always show Manhattan running up and down the page. But for a truer picture you need to tilt that map clockwise, just a shade. This whole thing is complicated by the fact that it's virtually impossible to use a magnetic compass because of all that high-rise metal interfering with polarity. If it's all making you feel a bit giddy, go down to the East Village (I prefer to call it the East-Southeast Village) where Stuyvesant Street (a one-off diagonal street) runs pretty accurately east to west.

GIVE YOUR COORDINATES BY LAMP-POST

Around town you don't want to be bothered with OS maps and grid references. But there's another very simple way to pinpoint an exact spot on a street. Just look at the lamp-posts as a highly visible system of location markers, covering your home town like a grid.

How it works

All lamp-posts are numbered, so that the public can report a faulty lamp. The numbers are highly visible, and usually on the street side of the post.

But best of all, they run in sequence from one end of the street to another, so you'll always know exactly where to find your target number. Suggested uses of lamp-post numbers are:

- To fix a precise location to meet, or to direct someone to a parked car.
- To identify a spot where house numbers are confusing (thus lamp-post numbers are used instead).
- To devise a lamp-post treasure hunt game.

Most councils have online maps of lamp-posts showing the numbers, which opens up a whole new range of possibilities for this urban resource. Search in the local directory under 'street lighting'.

Telegraph posts have numbers too, but the system is sometimes erratic.

TELLING THE TIME USING A SKY DISH

Boy scouts and all those in khaki shorts learn at an early age how to find north or south with a wristwatch and the angle of the sun. Then they promptly forget. But the point is that they know it can be done. What strikes me as odd about all of this is the assumption that a luckless traveller is bound to have with them either a watch or a compass. I guess if they hadn't mislaid their compass they wouldn't be lost in the first place. And if they were careless enough to lose their compass, chances are they can't really be trusted with a watch.

In urban bushcraft we're more realistic. You may well have neither compass nor watch, I accept that. Just as long as you can find a Sky dish, and make out the sun in the sky, it's not a problem. I've already explained how to find north with a satellite dish, and once you can do that you can tell the time too. All you have to do is just run that old wristwatch routine in reverse. It's quite a clever twist, I think.

1. Imagine a watch face on your wrist. Even draw on a 12 . . . it helps.
2. Use the Sky dish method to find south (see above).
3. Imagine the north–south line and a line from the sun meeting in the centre of your watch.
4. Make south the midpoint between the 12 and the hour.
5. The sun is now at the correct hour on your watch face.

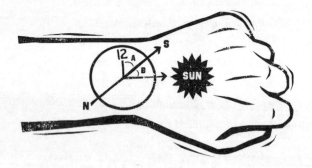

In the diagram the time is 3 o'clock.

NB. The angles at A and B are the same.

- During daylight saving (British Summer Time) use 1 instead of 12 o'clock.
- Southern hemisphere: point 12 o'clock towards the sun.
- Make N the midpoint between the sun and the correct hour of the day.

INSTANTLY SURVEY YOUR QUICKEST ROUTE

Walking around town there aren't too many opportunities to set a course straight for where you want to go. There's always lots of stuff in the way, like streets and tall buildings. But every now and then the opportunity presents itself to pursue a straight line. Crossing a playing field or a playground or a parking lot, places like that. This is where the urban bushman doesn't want to deviate the tiniest bit from the shortest possible route. And as any Roman road-builder will tell you, the shortest route is a straight line.

Most of us are familiar with the feeling. You've just walked across the park and you look back at your route. The evidence is clear and it's deeply upsetting. There was a perfectly clear straight route to take, but instead you meandered hither and thither, normally in a great big curve.

As you got nearer you could see that you were off course and tried to compensate, but at each turn it was too little too late. Why? Because the visual bearing you took on where you were heading was just a single marker, not two. You should know better than that. Time to start going straight.

From your start point, look at your final destination. There is a straight line between you and it. Now you need to find a way to mark out that line so that you can't deviate from it an inch. Here's how.

Pick a prominent point directly behind it or in front of it on the same straight line. That VW camper van in the car park, the clock tower behind, a goal-post in the park or a cooling tower beyond. Whatever you choose, the important thing is to keep this on the same line as you walk. Now, instead of wandering all over the place and still feeling you're heading straight, you'll know for sure. Ignore paths; they weren't designed with your pressing needs in mind.

A smarter way is to take a moment to fix several points on your straight path. Line up a gatepost railing with your objective. Now pick several objects on the route that you must pass.

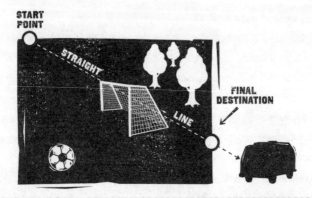

START POINT

STRAIGHT

LINE

FINAL DESTINATION

Urban bushcraft through the ages: Dr Who

It's not so much the Doctor I want to pay homage to, but that thing in his top pocket.

Doctor Who first appeared in 1968 when the computer age was looming and the space age was just beginning. We'd landed on the moon but it hadn't half been a struggle. In Houston giant spools of tape whizzed around at 100mph, *Mission Impossible* style, and worried controllers in thick-rimmed glasses stared at tiny monitor screens. It felt like we'd hauled ourselves to the edge of a precipice and now we were staring over the edge. Who knew what was out there?

The Doctor, that's who. He'd been thousands of years into the future and knew inside out the infinite possibilities of space. He'd seen the whole blueprint. He understood every discovery, every advance, forces we couldn't even contemplate. And the tool in his top pocket harnessed all of this potential. It was the sonic screwdriver.

To a generation of goggle-eyed boys this connected in a way only we could truly understand. It was obvious when you thought about it. Of course! Whether you need new batteries in your Hot Wheels Super Charger or a way to defeat the Daleks, it comes down to the same thing. Salvation is at hand so long as you can call on a grown-up with a screwdriver in his top pocket.

POSTING LETTERS THE LAZY WAY

End the frustration of unposted letters by getting a stranger to post them for you

Sending a letter by post is much harder than it sounds. The first part – writing it, filling in the form and enclosing the cheque – is fine. But it's the next bit that's the problem; the actual putting of the thing into the post-box. Even if you remember to take it with you, it's still in your bag days later, collecting smudges and wrinkles.

The trouble is that letters unposted turn into chores, drab nags in brown envelopes. Before email, when everything went by post, a trip to the post-box was part of daily life. There was joy in it because letters were different; white envelopes bulging with personality, addressed in five lines of hand-writing, cute and curly or slanted and intriguing.

If a letter was dropped in the street any decent person would pick it up, brush it off and send it on its way at the next post-box. Letters made a personal appeal to our sense of civic duty. And it's this realisation that the writer P.G. Wodehouse* abused (admirably) in a system for avoiding trips to the post-box altogether. Here it is:

1. Settle into an upstairs study overlooking a street.

2. Write letter.

3. Seal envelope, add address and stamp.

4. Open window.

5. Throw letter onto street below.

6. Sit back and await reply.

* In his memoirs *Bring on the Girls!*, Wodehouse boasted: 'it saves me going down four flights of stairs every time I want to mail a letter'. That's devilish enough, but we also know that the idea came from a friend, and he was just passing it off as his own. What ho, Wodehouse!

Wodehouse's flash of genius deserves to be revisited, so I've been trying it out. As long as you have the character and the courage to go through with it, it can still work over fifty years later. But there are a couple of tweaks that will improve your chances.

Although just tossing a letter out of the window has obvious appeal, I think the neighbours would get wise to it pretty soon. These days we need to work a bit harder. Here are the golden rules of pavement letter posting:

- A personal touch is paramount. Where possible, avoid brown envelopes and write addresses by hand. Even if an envelope is provided, add a personal touch (colourful special edition stamps help).
- Drop your letters in a visible spot on the pavement. Better still are garden walls, tables outside a cafe, posh shops, and best of all, a church pew. The research into this also suggests that dropping letters in affluent areas improves your chances of success.
- Expect a success rate of 50–60 per cent, so only send non-essential letters this way. Where possible, double up each letter and drop twice to improve your chance of success.

How it works

Over the years since Wodehouse, several very helpful psychological studies have added to our knowledge of what works best, together with how and why. In one study, for instance, all the letters were addressed to extremist political organisations. Not surprisingly, they had a lower success rate (30 per cent) than letters to individuals (70 per cent). Another experiment involved leaving letters on the bus or Tube, which was largely successful, but flawed; people would run after the experimenter to give them back the 'dropped' letter.

The most recent test on the streets of London had a success rate of 60 per cent, and similar tests in the US hit 55 per cent. Out of ten letters I 'posted' on a Bristol pavement, only two were lost (though they may still show up, of course).

Urban bushcraft through the ages: Ned Kelly

As a boy I loved the Wild West. Cowboys, Indians, Wyatt Earp, the whole lot. But something about *Butch Cassidy and the Sundance Kid* troubled me.

It wasn't the soft focus and Sacha Distel songs. There were other concerns for the 12-year-old critic, and chief among them was the final scene. Our sharp-shooting, quick-witted heroes are eventually cornered. With a couple of six guns and a handful of bullets they face the entire Bolivian army. This surely is time for their latest, greatest ingenious plan. But no! What's this? Instead of devising an ingenious getaway, they just run straight into a hail of rifle fire.

I expected more. Couldn't they find a cache of guns or discover a secret escape tunnel? Why not bribe a Bolivian, tie him up and walk out wearing his uniform? Clint would have known what to do.

Then I heard about Ned Kelly. They called him a bush ranger. But there was no dewy-eyed sentimentality about it. The 'bush' was just a place to hide between robbing banks.

Like Butch and Sundance, Ned ended up in an ambush, outgunned and surrounded. But this guy was well used to shooting his way out of trouble. He had dirt under his nails and a murderous look in his eye (Ned was Australian, so he didn't get the Hollywood makeover). For Ned this was just another day at the office and he approached it with chilling practicality.

This is what Ned did. He picked up a bucket, put it on his head and emerged shooting policemen at will. He wasn't sure if it would work. But it did. As long as he kept the rest of his body under cover he could pop up, gun blazing and those bullets bounced off the bucket like hailstones on a tin roof.

After my Butch and Sundance disappointment this felt like a coming of age. My heart hammered as Ned Kelly initiated me into the dirty reality of the adult world. There really was no magic solution, no showmanship or fast-talking trickery. At times all it came down to was stuff like this: a cold cast-iron bucket.

Ned pulled the same trick a few times. He got a blacksmith to fashion him a whole makeshift suit of armour. But the helmet was the crowning glory. Eventually the forces of law and order caught up with him, just as they did with Butch and Sundance. But Ned had distinguished himself. He had a plan; it wasn't pretty, but it worked.

3
THE HUMAN MULTI-TOOL

This special section eases you into the spirit of your new untamed approach to life by acquainting you with the toolkit you get issued with just by being human: your own body.

As you discover new ways to measure and record distance and time these techniques will be your constant companion. As well as helping you cope with some everyday dilemmas, they're great to pull out of the back pocket when you're travelling or when you have bored kids to entertain, or both.

DISTANCE AND TIME – ADVENTURES IN 4-D

To solve everyday problems you need to answer some everyday questions. These are the questions that run through our lives. You hear them quite a lot. And most of them involve measurements.

- How big is that sofa?
- How far away is that pub?

- How long will it take to get back to the car?
- How long have we lived here?
- How wide is the shelf?
- Will it fit?

Some people would be happy to just have a guess. Others would wait till they've got a tape measure/calendar/calculator/surveyor with them. But not you; not now.

With a bit of effort you can turn your body into a ready reckoner of scale that equips you to tackle any task in four dimensions. Oh yes, four. As well as handling 3-D you can measure time as well; your body comes with a clock, fitted as standard.

THE HUMAN RULER

What you need

Find a piece of string and a ruler or tape measure. As you work through each section make a note of your personal statistics and keep it somewhere handy, at least until you can remember all the most useful bits.

What it's for

Your aim is to build a system that turns your entire body into a finely calibrated gauge. When you can measure anything using bits of your body, there'll be no more need to remember where you put the tape measure. And that's good news when you need to measure up a piece of furniture, carpets, shelving ... stuff like that.

But this is just the start. You're about to create a four-dimensional toolkit that allows you to calculate much longer distances. You'll be able to tell how far away you are from just about anything, how fast or slow you're going ... and more.

It's a habit-forming system that gets better and more accurate the more you practise. Early human systems of measurement were all based on anatomical proportions. Now you are reclaiming that concept, linking cold abstract ideas to warm and familiar flesh.

> **The traditional measure** of an inch is the width of a thumb at the bottom of the nail. In French the word for inch and thumb is the same. As it is in Italian, Swedish, Dutch and Sanskrit . . .

How it works

Use your body's natural dimensions as a measuring machine. The width of a thumb, the span of your hand, the length from elbow to tip of index finger (that one is actually the ancient measurement of one cubit). It's best to find the bits of your body that have a memorable whole number measurement.

You may even luck out and find some useful decimal lengths. A good one to start looking for is 10cm. Maybe it's the length of a fingertip to the knuckle, or the width of five fingers, the distance between mole A and mole B. Have fun with a ruler and track it down, preferably somewhere you can access fairly easily. Knuckles, elbows and knees are useful fixed points.

Now do the same with other distances from 5cm up to 50cm. To find a metre you can use several spans (splayed fingers from thumb to tip of little finger). But the best way is to measure from the tip of the nose to your hand with it stretched out to the side. This is the ancient measure of one yard. It's good for measuring rope and line. If it's not quite long enough, turn your head to one side to gain a few more inches.

You need to be as accurate as possible. To reduce the margin for error I use a system of averages. For instance, measure four hand spans and divide by four, rather than just measuring it once.

EGYPTIAN MEASUREMENTS

One digit = the width of a finger

Four digits = one palm

Three palms = a small span

Fourteen digits = a large span

Twenty-eight digits = seven palms = one cubit

One cubit = the length from tip of index finger to elbow

Measure your 'wingspan' – from fingertip to fingertip with arms outstretched. This is a fathom. It's also the same as your height (give or take a centimetre or two to allow for your freaky variations from normality).

THE REAL DA VINCI CODE

We're built with beautiful symmetry, so we may as well use it. Classical artists made a science of the system of related proportions to which all our bodies conform. Leonardo da Vinci knew all about it (along with most other mysterious secrets of the universe). But right now it's just handy. It helps you to build a consistent set of measurements that's instantly memorable.

'Nature has thus arranged the measurements of a man: four fingers make one palm and four palms make one foot; six palms make one cubit; four cubits make once a man's height; four cubits make a pace, and twenty-four palms make a man's height . . .'

Leonardo da Vinci (1452–1519)

SIZE OF A COW

In cricket, a bowler instinctively knows if the distance between the wickets 'looks' right. He's used to it. He has that 22-yard pitch marked out in his mind's eye. So cricketers should gauge longer distances on a scale of 22 yards. If you've got five cricket pitches to go till you're there, that's 110 yards.

Now find your own equivalent. You can already picture the length of your street pretty accurately, the width of your garden or the height of your house. So just put them to use. Measure them and store them away as standard measures.

The well-prepared urban bushman can call on most everyday objects to use as measuring tools. If none are available, consider the waistband of your trousers (look for the size in the label). I've also used a size-16 shirt collar as a measuring tape.

Other useful objects to know the measurements of are:

2p coin	1 inch across
Credit card	2 inches wide
£20 note	3 inches wide
Bic/Biro	15cm/6in long
Guitar	one yard from end to end
Broom handle	standard length is 120cm, though can be 110–130cm
Cow	(adult Friesian) 240cm
Small car (Mini)	371cm
Big car (Mondeo estate)	480cm

The last two longer lengths come into play now, with a handy system for judging distance.

THE THUMB-OMETER
Measuring long distance by thumb

Having mastered things you can measure by hand, we move on to things that call for a craftier calculation; all those distances you can't measure, like from here to the car, the pub, the next bus stop, that skyscraper on the horizon, that plane in the sky.

This way of measuring is an ancient system, the original rule of thumb.

And it's a valuable part of anyone's urban survival toolkit. It involves doing a small sum, but the results are well worth any amount of arithmetic.

There is very little that can go wrong here as long as you obey one essential rule. Don't mix up your metric and imperial; pick a unit of measurement and stick to it.

Stretch out your arm and stick up your thumb. Now close one eye and blot out an object in the distance. Once initiated in the numerology of thumbs, you can work out how far you (and your thumb) are from that object. All you need is one magic number. It holds the answer to the thumb, the universe and everything. And that number is . . . 30.

THE HUMAN MULTI-TOOL **99**

Let me explain. With your arm outstretched, the distance between your thumb and your eye is (approximately) 30 thumb widths. That's it. It all flows from there.

AN EXAMPLE

I hold out my arm, with my thumb held on its side, horizontally. A distant car appears to be half the height of my thumb's width. Here comes the sum. I know cars are generally 5ft high, so my thumb appears to be 10ft wide. I now just multiply 10 by that magic number of 30. The result is 300 – and so the car is 300ft from my thumb.

The formula is this: distance = apparent size of thumb compared to distant object × 30.

Try it – it works on anything. To test it out start by standing about 30ft from something that's one foot high. Or 30m from something a metre high. Your thumb should completely cover it. At half the distance you need two thumb widths to cover it.

To make this work all you need is an idea of the standard measurements of the kind of stuff you'll see in your urban habitat. Cars tend to be 5ft high, a classic black taxi is 15ft long, a single storey of a building is 10 to 12ft high, and a standard London double-decker bus is about 29ft long (9m) and 8ft (2.4m) wide. Oh, and passenger planes tend to be about 150ft (40m) from tip to tail.

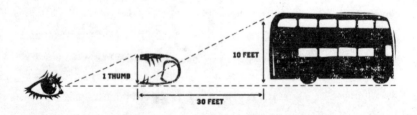

My outstretched thumb appears to blot out a bus. The bus is 10ft high, so I know it's 300ft away.

- Be careful to keep your units of measurements consistent. Whatever you use for the distant object will be the same for the resulting distance.
- For larger things use a fist. The magic number now is 6 (your outstretched arm is 6 fist widths long); for smaller objects use half a thumb, and double the number. Instead of 30, it's 60.

How it works

It's all to do with triangles, and that beautiful gift of proportion.

What you're doing is making two similar triangles: a short one from your eye to your thumb, and another from your thumb to the object. You know the angles are all the same and have enough of the measurements to fill in some gaps.

And the number 30 comes into it because although we are all different sizes we are all in proportion. The relative size of our thumbs (and fists) to the length of our arms tends to be the same – and with your thumb outstretched it's 30 thumb widths from your eye.

WINKING DISTANCE

There's another way of doing the same thing by winking. All you need to know here is that the distance between your eyes is about a tenth of the length of your arm. So this time what you need to do is put your thumb out, and with one eye shut line up the nail with one edge of the object. Now swap eyes and your thumb will seem to shift position. Using what you know about the size of a bus, or a cow, figure out how far your thumb appears to have moved.

If it moved two bus lengths, and a bus is about 30ft long, it moved 60ft. Now multiply that by your new magic number: 10. You'll end up with the distance from thumb to bus. I make that 600ft. That's 200 yards to most of us.

PACE YOURSELF

A formula for measuring distance and speed

This is a system for working out your walking speed, as you go. It comes to us from our old friend Sir Francis Galton. It does what a GPS might do for you, but it's always a joy to show that stuff like this didn't start with the invention of pocket-sized gadgets in black and silver.

Sir Francis would have used the formula to calculate travel time between river and native village or from camp to the next volcano. Here, it's more likely to serve in finding out whether we'll be at the church on time, the cinema before the film starts or the pub before closing time.

All you need to know is the length of your average pace. Then you can keep the GPS on your mobile phone firmly in your pocket. Though feel free to use the calculator function to do the required little bit of working out.

First you need to measure your average stride length (l). The best thing to do is measure out a hundred yards (on a football pitch or running track). Count how many strides you take (n), then divide 100 by that number (100/n = l) to find the average pace length.

Say somebody tells you to walk for half a mile then turn left after the electricity substation. It only takes a minute or two before you start to have doubts. Have you gone too far? Did you miss it? That's when you're tempted to see if the GPS on your phone can help you to figure out how far you've gone. But with this system you can tell straightaway. You're walking at 6mph, so it will take you 5 minutes.

Once you have this length of your average pace, refer to the magic table below, in which Sir Francis worked out, for all stride lengths, how many seconds (s) it would take to make ten paces, travelling at 1mph. This is the golden ticket; one figure that allows you to always work out how fast you're going.

Shaded column shows stride lengths in inches

21	11.9	31	17.6	41	23.3
22	12.5	32	18.2	42	23.9
23	13.1	33	18.4	43	24.4
24	13.7	34	19.3	44	25.0
25	14.3	35	19.9	45	25.6
26	14.8	36	20.5	46	26.1
27	15.4	37	21.1	47	26.7
28	15.9	38	21.6	48	27.3
29	16.4	39	22.2	49	27.8
30	17.0	40	22.8	50	28.4

The personal pace calculator

Now, taking this magic number as your personal speed counter, this is what you do:

- Find your pace length on the chart and look for your personal 'magic number' of seconds.
- Count the number of paces you take in that number of seconds and divide it by 10.
- If it is 10 paces, you're bang on 1mph. If 20, then 2mph, if it's 40 or 50 paces . . . then it's 4 or 5mph.
- More practically, this doesn't often come to round figures. But the formula works to one decimal place and the sums are hardly tough. For instance: my pace length is

34 inches, so my magic number is 19.3. In that time I
count 38 paces. I just divide 38 by 10, to discover I'm
walking at a relaxed 3.8mph.

If you forget the second number but still have your pace length, then here's another simple formula to give you your speed over the ground.

- You need to know how many steps (n) you take in
  5.7 seconds (walk for 17 seconds and divide it by 3).
- Now multiply the number of steps (n) by the length (l)
  of the pace in inches and divide the answer by 100. The
  formula is nl/100. For instance, let's say I walk 38 paces
  in 17 seconds. That's 12.6 in 5.7 seconds.
- My pace length is 40 inches. $40 \times 12.6 / 100 = 5$.
  I'm walking at 5mph.

AT A NAIL'S PACE

There are certain events in life that deserve a monument more personal than an entry in a calendar, and more enduring than a scrawled note in biro on the back of your hand.

With a thumbnail clock you can give singular meaning and worldly gravitas to the passing of time. The ancients had their stone circles and the phases of the moon. Now you can watch the days ebb away at the same speed that continents drift apart. Blimey.

To make a thumbnail clock

This technique has a whole load of potential applications. The most commonplace way of making it is to score your nail at the cuticle to mark a major event in your life, something like moving house, starting a job or pulling off a spectacular three-dart checkout. To get kids involved try

Urban bushcraft through the ages: Doctor William Bean

When I first heard about William Bean's fingernail clock I wondered how long he'd been in prison. Staring at four walls for years can lead men to do great things. The storybooks are full of this kind of thing. For a start, there's Casanova's epic escape from prison in Venice using a chisel he'd made from a door bolt. Then there's the birdman of Alcatraz and his 35-year study of diseases of the sparrow. And who could forget the officers of the 51st Highland Division, who used their time in a German POW camp to invent a new country dance.

But then I found out that Doctor William B. Bean had been a free man all his life, a life devoted to the study of fingernail growth. What a guy.

He started his study in 1941. In 1976 he published his magnum opus: *Nail Growth: 35 Years of Investigation.* It's been called the most boring scientific study ever. But in fact it's one of the most thrilling; as you'll soon see.

In 1941 Dr Bean scratched a line on his thumbnail just above the cuticle and set about timing its progress towards the tip. Then he developed a special system. He'd tattoo his thumbnail each month at the point it emerged and use a specially made gauge to measure its growth. He soon branched out to fingers and toenails too.

Dr Bean's revelations are still the last word on the subject. He found the daily rate of growth of the thumbnail is 0.123mm, with no seasonal variation, and it's staggeringly constant over a lifetime. But this is the bit I love. When he got ill with mumps, his nails slowed down to a halt. Then, when he got better, the growth rate almost doubled, as if to make up for lost time. For all these beautiful revelations, Dr Bean, we salute you.

making a mark when they start at a new school. No one else in class will have a watch like this. Or they could do it at the same time with all the members of the playground secret agent club. OK guys, synchronise thumbs.

On the first day of your new era, file a furrow along the bottom of the nail, where it emerges from the cuticle. Now you are going to make a device that allows you to take accurate measurements as it progresses up the nail with the reliable constancy of any atomic clock.

You need a matchbox, some graph paper or any calibrated scale, and some glue.

A thumbnail clock

1. Remove the matchbox 'tray' and cut off one end.
2. Now place the digit to be monitored into the open end, all the way so that the tip rests against the other end. For extra precision draw a line around it so that you can put it back in the exact same position each time.
3. Cut away enough of the matchbox's sliding 'lid' to reveal the whole nail length, but leaving the sides of the nail hidden.
4. Stick your measuring gauge or graph paper to the remaining sides. These are now the 'gauge' and should rest nicely along the length of the nail.

The clock is now ready. Using the Bean constant of 0.123mm per day you can mark 10-day periods along the gauge. Or each time you take a measurement use the constant to calculate the elapsed number of days.

THE THUMBNAIL COUNTDOWN

Here's a thumbnail timer that doesn't depend on building the clock. This technique is for when you want a constant reminder of approaching events. If you're lucky enough to have a thumbnail that's around 1.2cm long you will be able to follow a mark as it travels the whole length of your nail, and to know when 100 days has passed. But for most of us it's safer to mark 100-day periods in reverse, from the top of the nail down.

Take care to measure from where the 'white' of the nail tip starts, rather than from the tip itself. This allows you to carry on cutting your nails without upsetting the calibration.

Just make a mark on your nail at 1.2cm down, 100 days before the big day, and watch your deadline approaching.

This is an especially good way of reminding yourself about nasty stuff. I use it to watch the approach of the 31 January tax deadline. The impending dark clouds are brightened by the joy of watching the process work. It softens the blow.

CHILDREN'S COUNTDOWN TIMER

If you can get children involved, this is a great way to deal with the endless questioning about how long there is until a birthday or Christmas . . .

In my experience, the questions begin to intensify with about a month to go. So to nip them in the bud, just measure your child's nail, and using the 0.1mm-a-day rule, make a mark at a spot 5mm or (50 days) from the end. Done. The answer to their question is on hand, literally, whenever they want to check.

NAIL GROWTH IN ORDER OF SPEED (FASTEST FIRST)

Thumb
Finger
Big toe
Other toes

4.
CITY-CENTRE
ADVENTURES

Every tribe mourns its past, and we city dwellers are no different. We liked things the way they were; we always have. But there's a difference between a fondness for the familiar and plain pig-headed resistance to change; that's a dead end you don't want to go down. Adapting to new habitats and new surroundings is what we do best, and besides, it's what urban bushcraft is all about.

One pet hate of the anti-progress league is the modern high street with its homogeneous shop fronts and multiple chain stores. They're all the same, they say. And indeed they are, well spotted you lot. But instead of moaning and signing petitions, the urban bushman sees all this as a big fat opportunity. Instead of getting worn down by the queues and the lack of a place to pee, he grasps this chance to do what he does best; to rise above the herd and strike out on his own.

Amid the bored shoppers along the high street and the mind-altering marketing messages of the mall he can craft a city-centre adventure. By retuning the tribal antenna, he blocks out the big branded bribes and picks up the timeless wisdom beneath. This, after all, is his domain; from the cheese aisle to the customer services counter and the cash till to the coffee shop; it's what thousands of years of progress have been leading to, and now's the time to make the most of it. Let's go to town.

HOW TO PREDICT THE WEATHER WITH A CUP OF COFFEE

This is an ageless technique that's especially satisfying when you pull it off among the laptops and body piercings of a 21st-century coffee shop.

A mall is a good place to practise some earth science, and a coffee break is a good time to check the likelihood of rain. If you've just dashed in for shelter, then this should help you decide whether to make a beeline for the bus before it gets worse, or relax and order another while the skies clear. Of course, you could just listen out for an up-to-date weather report, but then you could just drink instant coffee, and you don't. This is lifestyle weather forecasting.

Back in the America of the Waltons, this way of predicting the weather was as familiar as dungarees and moonshine.

- Take a cup of black coffee (made from beans).
- Drop a lump of sugar to the bottom of the cup.
- Don't stir or disturb the coffee.
- Watch the bubbles rise to the surface.
- Notice where bubbles gather.

How to read your coffee barometer:

- Bubbles in the middle: FINE WEATHER.

- Bubbles around the rim: RAIN OR SNOW.
- Bubbles all over the place: CHANGEABLE.

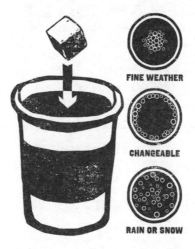

How it works

The tiny air bubbles in the sugar lump are released as the sugar dissolves. The high pressure that keeps the skies clear and the weather fair pushes down on the centre of the coffee, making the surface curve down at the middle, so the bubbles hit the middle first and gather there.

Low pressure, indicating clouds and rain, works like a vacuum, pulling up the centre of the drink, so the bubbles gather at the edges.

The behaviour of the bubbles in the fluid is particular to coffee and is caused by the surface tension and slight oiliness from the beans.

TIPS

- Don't try this in *frappé*-style iced drinks. The heat of the coffee improves the performance – something to do with surface tension.

- Milk is the enemy of the reliable barometer. We're not looking for froth here but for those tiny golden bubbles you get in a rich black coffee. The best weather forecasters drink either Americano or a simple espresso.

FOR MINI METEOROLOGISTS

Set up restless children with their own weather station in an espresso cup. Get them to make observations as they drop in a lump of sugar every five minutes, to be repeated three times. It should keep them busy while you catch up on the sports section. That's quarter of an hour to study the form while they learn an essential life skill.

THE FESTIVAL FORECAST

These days, whether it's Glastonbury, Isle of Wight or Womad, you can't move for coffee stalls. Win points by forecasting what the weather will be like by the time the headline act is on the main stage.

CAUGHT IN THE RAIN?

- The down-draught heater in shop doorways makes a good dryer for hair and shoulders – it hits you from above, so gets to all the same parts as the rain.
- Supermarket layout considerations dictate that they must have an entry area where customers are encouraged to linger while they are introduced to the shop environment. It's where the newspapers and flowers are kept. This is the best place to loiter and stay dry, without shopping. It's what it's there for.

THE SPECIAL FORCES APPROACH TO CUSTOMER COMPLAINTS

Elite training in the secret techniques for cracking the call centre

Calling customer services is one of the toughest tests of nerve that modern life has to offer. So naturally it's an irresistible opportunity for the urban bushman to practise his art. First, let's study what's going on.

On the other end of the phone there's a mindless automaton reading from a script. Then, if you get past them, you face the well-drilled specialist with pat responses that deflect all your questions until you lose the will to live. This is a one-on-one confrontation, a mental chess game where you have to

The Special Forces system can be applied to any customer-services confrontation; insurance companies, mortgage lenders, mobile phone operators or a customer-complaints desk.

Life as a consumer is generally fairly straightforward. But then something goes wrong and it all changes; you've been overcharged, blatantly ripped off or misled, and you need to phone up and complain. And suddenly life turns into a scene in an airport thriller.

The clock ticks. Beads of sweat jostle for position on your forehead. You stare at the phone and it stares right back. All you can think about is making the call. You pick it up and start to dial. You've done this ten times already, only this time you won't hang up; you'll see it through to the end.

Click. The phone answers and you wait for the dreaded voice. You flinch, here it comes: 'For questions about your bill and all other enquiries . . .' You press 2 just to make it stop. Another beep . . . 'All of our representatives are busy. Please wait while we connect your call . . .' Your strength is fading.

You want to give up, but you have to go on. Then it happens . . . it's the hold music. No, please . . . anything but that!

hold firm while your opponent does all they can to grind you down.

What's needed here is a system to give you the strength to endure and help you to keep your goal in sight. That's what I was looking for when the answer hit me. It was shining straight at me like a spotlight in a bare cell: the SAS anti-interrogation drill.

'Anti-interrogation' is an SAS speciality. On top-secret missions behind enemy lines there's always a chance of capture so it's essential they don't crack under questioning. In training, SAS soldiers are drilled in the seven essentials of anti-interrogation. And with a bit of minor adaptation this same code of conduct can become a guide to customer complaints that'll turn you into a call-centre maestro. The symmetry between the two scenarios is uncanny. Whether you're an SAS soldier facing a gruelling interrogation or the urban bushman calling a complaints line, this is the best briefing you'll get.

RULE 1

SAS: Accept the situation you're in; you're likely to suffer, and it will be a long process.
Urban bushman: Don't be put off by the cheesy music, the jargon and the recorded messages; resolve to see your money-back mission through to the end.

RULE 2

SAS: Keep your mental integrity – it's the one thing you can control.
Urban bushman: Don't ever say 'Actually it's fine, I'm probably just being fussy.'

RULE 3

SAS: Be 'the grey man'. Never get aggressive or stand out.
Urban bushman: Don't be rude or snippy, keep the moral high ground.

RULE 4

SAS: Beware of a switch to softer tactics and claims that they're just trying to help you. This is designed to make you talk.

Urban bushman: If they start calling you 'sir' and offering apologies from the manager don't buckle, stick to your demands.

RULE 5

SAS: Overplay any injuries they cause you, even cry.

Urban bushman: Maintain your outrage at every stage of the process. Make sure they know how inconvenient all this is. Complain about the frustration of waiting on hold.

RULE 6

SAS: Use eye-to-eye contact. Make them identify with you.

Urban bushman: Get the name of the rep you're dealing with, and use it. Ask them directly for help; a personal element can work where all else fails.

RULE 7

SAS: 'What if . . .' Plan ahead and be ready to react if things change.

Urban bushman: Prepare your responses for any eventuality. Be ready for them to make a token offer or reject your complaint or refer you to head office . . . don't let them surprise you into agreeing anything.

THE MALL OF THE WILD

The mall is a machine for turning people into shoppers. First it unsettles us with its anodyne atmosphere, then it lures us in with a powerful piece of tribal persuasion. Once he's understood the forces at work, the urban bushman can have fun dodging their grasp.

To do that, though, we need to understand how the two-part process works.

PART ONE: THE NOMAD IN THE MALL

The old-fashioned street with lamp-posts and a gutter is a place where people feel at home. It's somewhere to flirt and burp and do as you please. But how different things are when we hit the mall. On the face of it this place is designed for our comfort and delight, with its fountain-side piazzas and coffee-bar atriums. But nobody ever feels at home here, do they? Not really. I always think shoppers in malls have the look of an uninvited horde at a glitzy wedding. You can see it in their eyes; they're trying to blend in, but failing.

Think about it like this: if you had a football on the street you'd give it a few bounces. If there weren't any cars coming you'd even have a kick-about. On the street you can tie up your dog, chain up your bike and act as you please. But not in the mall, not ever.

It all comes down to the big central purpose; this place is for shopping in. Like a motorway services or an airport, it's where people are processed; they become a throughput, never a population. In the mall we're nomads, we can't settle, and that's a pretty soulless experience for a territorial animal like man.* At least in an airport there's that little room where you can go and pray (far better value than the first-class lounge, by the way). In the mall there's nothing for it but to shop, and so you're ready for part two.

PART TWO: THE TRIBAL TRAP

Back when our tribal village was just a hundred strong it was important to show we knew the rules and that we'd fit in just fine. We needed everyone to know that we were on the level, and over the centuries it became a habit.

* Next time you go to a mall, try this. Claim a bit of territory by setting up camp just like at the airport when you're waiting for a delayed departure. Take turns to make shopping forays and come back to base. Now doesn't that feel better? Told you.

Nowadays, most of the people that surround us are completely irrelevant to our lives, but we still like them to think we're part of the gang. It's just another survival strategy that's outlived its purpose. And it comes to the fore in the mall. Softened up and unsettled, we're at our most shallow and vulnerable. Then we're offered membership of a club, a tribal identity and a way to fit in with the crowd, so we grab it.

Every retailer on the high street works hard at telling us that buying makes us belong. It's why shops create a mood, a lifestyle to aspire to. Membership is formalised with a flurry of rituals, little branded blessings if you like, all giving the process an inflated over-importance. Your purchase is adoringly wrapped, then there's the congratulatory chit-chat, and finally comes the oversized shopping bag with its handles of silken cord. A little sticky fastener at the top seals the deal and you're ready to go, sent out like a missionary to spread the good word.

The best and simplest demonstration of all this is the tribalism at work in the market for fast food and coffee on the go, where the badge of belonging is a bright yellow burger box or a branded paper cup. Here's how it works.

Professor Latte

Bryant Simon from Philadelphia's Temple University has studied why people buy coffee at Starbucks prices when they really don't need to. He breaks the reasons into three categories: the 'functional' (serving a coffee addiction); the 'emotional' (giving ourselves a treat); and, for him the most powerful, the 'expressive' (showing the world we can afford luxury). Before you know it, Starbucks is issuing branded paper cups to six million people a day, all desperate to tell the world they belong.

Starbuckers

Starbuckers (as I call them) feel comfortable in their club because of a strictly policed demographic profile; this is a sanctuary for the comfortably off in their late teens to mid-40s, and nobody else dares enter. The oldies are seen off by the decor, the music and the pierced eyebrows of the servers while the high price of a coffee keeps away the spotty youths and the buy-rite brigade in cheap clothing.

We are all suckers for some tribal seduction and an open invitation to belong. But we aren't complete mugs. A logo and a shop front alone isn't enough to have us clamouring to enlist. We want to be wooed with a bit of hoodoo, some ritual, and some exciting new language. So that's just what the high street's biggest brands give us. Starbucks or McDonald's, Argos or Pret; just walk in and you're under the spell of the tribal language, the customs, the music and the brand. Skinny lattes, oddly shaped trays, stubby little pens, happy meals . . . It's a hypnotic ritual conducted by witchdoctors in green aprons or red caps, and the Stone Age brain instantly wants to be in on it . . . Look over there! Who's that loser who doesn't know where the coffee stirrers are?

The art of not belonging

This is a simple way of restating your identity in the mall. I use it as a kind of reboot whenever the urge to buy into the brands gets too strong. And it's a good demonstration of how strong the tribal persuasion can be.

The moment of ordering is the key to tribal belonging. By using that special language, you're swearing allegiance and joining the club. It's a little piece of theatre that bonds you to the brand.

Now think how it would feel to go into McDonald's and calmly order a pizza, with extra mushrooms. Or ask a pierced barista in Starbucks for a chicken chow mein? If you don't think you could do it, all the more reason to try. If nothing else, it will give you a ten-second rush of adrenaline, like a mini bungee jump.

Here's what you do:

- First select your target; the kind of place that puts employees in uniforms and uses the TM logo on words they've made up on the menu. Starbucks works well on all counts.
- Once you've picked your spot, don't hesitate. Just walk in and wait to be served.
- When you get to the front of the queue, look the assistant in the eye and calmly and politely ask for A CHEESEBURGER WITH FRIES.
- They may pretend they didn't hear or ask you to repeat it, so ask again. Say it as if it's the most natural thing in the world: CHEESEBURGER WITH FRIES PLEASE.
- When they tell you they don't have any, just thank them and leave.

As you head for the door, feel the excitement build. You did it. You broke the power of the tribe. You felt the pressure to conform and you defied it. And the best bit is that nobody's about to cast you into the wilderness. That's because it wasn't really a tribal ceremony at all, just a coffee chain wanting to charge over £2 for a cup of foamy milk.

Obviously if you do this too much you'll start to be branded as a loon, which does nobody any good.

Sock solutions

You're walking home from the supermarket and the handles of your carrier bags have turned to cheese wire. They've cut furrows across your fingers that make you want to cry, with half a mile to go and no bus in sight. Don't worry, comfy grip relief can be yours. Just take off a sock and wind it around the handle; it works a treat.

Those junk 'flyers' that fall out of newspapers are useful for this too (and for nothing else).

The white coffee challenge

Here's another version of the same thing; it's simpler but still fun. Go into any big coffee chain with a friend and order a drink without using any words from their special lexicon. They speak English don't they? Try asking for a 'white coffee' for instance. If you manage to get your drink without using any of the forbidden words during the entire exchange with staff, your friend pays.

Mission milk

The milk at a supermarket is always at the back, in the far corner. The idea is that you'll be distracted on the way and find yourself with a trolley full of premium-priced goodies. It's passive manipulation of your mind, and your wallet. Your mission, should you choose to accept it, is to buy a single carton of milk, and nothing else. If you succeed congratulate yourself on your resolve. This country needs people the likes of you.

TOILET WISDOM

Sooner or later you're going to have to find a loo. We all know that department stores, public libraries and bookshops are a more comfortable bet than bus stations and public toilets on the street. You probably have your own network of preferred sites, but here are a couple of tips.

THE UPGRADE

Think about it: every hotel has facilities somewhere near reception, and the doorman has no idea who's staying there or not. (Yes, I said doorman. We're not talking about the local Travelodge here.) Pick a big hotel, as swanky as you like. If it's a tourist hotel, big shopping bags and cameras help you blend in. If it's a businessman's favourite then make an effort to blend in. This all suits the urban bushman because it's a bit like getting an upgrade on a plane; play the part, pull it off with panache and your reward is a touch of first-class comfort.

I find this especially useful at train stations, where the big Sheraton or Hilton always has an international cast of hundreds milling around looking for their colleague. Instead of looking for Wayne from marketing, you're desperately seeking something else, but who'd really know.

CUBICLE CHOICE

Psychologists tend to agree than in public toilets there is a tendency to go to the cubicle furthest from the door first. As a result, the nearest cubicle is usually the cleanest and least used. If this were a dog race, your money should be on trap one.

Urban bushcraft through the ages: Tony Benn MP

'Pipe smoker' and 'wartime pilot' are both first-rate items for any chap's CV, doubly so when the name of the game is quick thinking and a flair for all things practical.

The politician and diarist Tony Benn can boast both. Clearly he is ideal urban bushman material, as he proved when he was caught short while driving in central London. With no toilets within striking distance, he had to think quickly, and he did. His solution was both ingenious and charmingly simple. And I for one will make sure it lives on. Here's what this great parliamentarian did. He pulled over, and having first adjusted his flies (I presume), climbed out of the car, opened the bonnet and leant over the engine as if peering at some troublesome part right at the back. As he let nature take its course, his cover was so good that he wasn't even rumbled when a passer-by commented that he could see what the problem was – a leaking radiator.

I suspect this method of emergency relief is best tried only by people of a certain height, with a good working knowledge of engines (or at least the parts that get hot).

THE CASHPOINT QUEUE (AND HOW TO JUMP IT)

The queue for the cashpoint is a special case because of three little quirks all of its own. You need to know this, whether you're planning to push in or simply defending your rightful place.

A. THE MULTIPLE QUEUE DECEPTION

With two or more cashpoints, the norm is to form a single queue, so that the person at the front goes to the first machine that's free. But it's only a convention, not a rule, and as a result this queue is at risk from the suggestion that each cashpoint should have a queue of its own.

Tactics

Let's start with the easiest target of all; a single person waiting in a queue of one when there's more than one cashpoint. Just draw an imaginary line between the cashpoints across the pavement and see which side of it the person is standing (person waiting). Very calmly take your position alongside them, on the other side of this line (you).

As far as they know, you simply assumed that there are two queues, one for each cashpoint. As there's not a lot at stake they're unlikely to argue. If challenged, this is easy to pass off as a simple mistake. Where more cashpoints are available this manoeuvre is easier still.

Bad positioning – unclear.

Defence – to prevent any ambivalence, adopt a wide stance firmly in the middle of the machine.

B. THE COURTESY GAP

Convention dictates that the first in line leaves a 'courtesy gap' behind the person at the cashpoint so that they don't feel threatened or overlooked. But this can be misinterpreted by people joining the queue. On crowded pavements it's normal to allow passing pedestrians through this gap, adding to the uncertainty (see picture below).

Tactics

If the courtesy gap is too large, stand between this person and the cashpoint, as if you hadn't seen them. Avoid eye contact. There's a good chance they'll avoid any confrontation and simply move in behind you. As above, this is easily passed off as a simple mistake.

Defence

Keep the courtesy gap no larger than 1.5m. Person waiting was there first, but you are able to move in easily owing to multiple queue deception and the courtesy gap being too large.

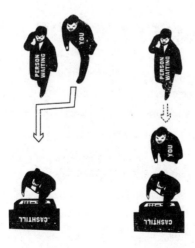

C. FRIENDS IN THE SAME QUEUE

When people stand in a queue with others who may or may not be taking out money, it's hard to judge who's in the queue and who isn't.

Opportunity: this always causes confusion so there's a chance to queue in front of one or both, on the supposed assumption that they're just waiting for a friend.

DEFENSIVE POSTURES

This simple code deters anyone with an eye on your place in the queue.

- Sideways stance: This allows you to hold a place and face down any challenger (see illustration below).
- Eye contact: A shrewd challenger avoids eye contact; don't let them escape it.
- Micro movements: The slightest shuffle can signal your intentions and make clear how the queue is working; normally enough to warn off any potential challenger.

THE SECRET LIFE OF A QUEUE

Queuing is something humans do all over the world, without a second thought. If you weren't particularly switched on, you could see it as a great civilising force, a system of cooperation held together by a shared sense of natural justice. But the urban bushman knows better than that and doesn't believe it for a second. Once you know the truth about this strange convention, then exploring it further is impossible to resist . . . especially where it can be turned to our advantage.

> **Just as there are little tricks** you can train animals to do to demonstrate a simple piece of behaviour, so there are with humans. Put a woodlouse in the light and he'll run towards darkness. Draw a chalk line across an ant's trail and he won't cross it. Start a queue in front of human beings and some of them will join it. Try it with a few friends. Just form a queue in front of a shop or market stall and see how long it is before people start to join the end.

THE LAW OF QUEUES

I didn't use to push in. But then I had a revelation, standing in the queue at a crowded airport check-in. There were tour groups and luggage trolleys everywhere, but at least it was a queue, so there was some sense of order. Then suddenly everything changed as a sea of people rushed to join a newly opened check-in lane. A family of seven that was way behind me in the original queue was now way up there in front. In fact the whole queue seemed to be comprised of people who were once back where I was. Now they were up there, where I wasn't. And nobody complained. First come, first served? Forget it. This was a perfect demonstration of the secret code of queues.

Rule 1: There are no rules

Queues pretend to be all about fair play, upholding the rule of first come, first served. But that's not how it is. That's just how we like things to look until there's a chance to get to the front. When it breaks down, the queue's real nature is revealed; it's every man for himself. In the airport nobody expects the queue to split fairly and move across to the newly opened lane in nice orderly sections. Anyone who can get to the front is applauded. They saw an opening and they took it.

This is one of many wrinkles in the system that has developed over the millennia since Noah made his animals go in two by two. We think of queue jumpers as the enemy, the rotten apples in the barrel, but if you pick your moment and take your chance, queue jumping can be seen as a noble art.

THE SEVEN SECRETS OF PUSHING IN

Psychologists love queues and love testing our behaviour when we're in them, which all goes to provide a pretty good guide to pushing in. Nearly all the studies show that people who push in aren't challenged as often as you might think. And by digging a bit deeper, you start to discover what tactics increase the chances of getting away with it. It's a valuable resource that is best remembered as seven secrets.

Single file

Single-file queues, where people stand one behind another, are the best for pushing in. In these queues, social order is weaker because there's no eye contact. Just slide in and stand facing forwards.

In a long queue, then, look for any part of it where people are standing in single file.

Excuse me

Of all the experiments relating to queues, the one in the 1980s by American psychologist Stanley Milgram recorded the lowest rate of complaints about blatant pushing in – constantly below 50 per cent and sometimes as low as 10 per cent. Ask yourself: if you knew there was only a 10 per cent chance of someone saying something, would you go for it? Me too. So here's the secret. As they pushed in, all of Milgram's line jumpers just said, 'Excuse me, I'd like to get in here', and stood in line, facing forward.

Back is best

The best hunting ground is towards the back. Though there's less to gain, success is far more likely. At the front, people become a tight-knit clique, likely to notice an impostor. But at the back, it's all far less organised, and far less suspicious too (people expect queue jumpers to target the front).

For all they know, someone who merges with confidence could be returning to their rightful spot. Join the line confidently a third of the way from the back and you'll soon be accepted as one of them.

Be first

Don't push in where others have done so already, as there's a much higher chance of people objecting. A one-off is sometimes accepted, but multiples rarely are. It's all because a queue accepts a certain amount of law breaking, on the basis that once the law breaker is in the queue the correct order is restored, and the queue becomes stronger. But if lots of people try it on, the whole queue could break down and people are forced to say something.

Bide your time

A queue assumes that the longer somebody's been waiting the more they deserve a reward. But time keeping can be a bit vague and it doesn't take too long before someone who has just shown up in a queue can start to accumulate points and be seen as a descrving case. If you push in, it sometimes takes only ten or fifteen minutes of waiting before you too are seen as a valid member of the queue, sharing the pain of waiting with those who might have been there for hours.

The brace

Queuing's painful because we see it as time down the toilet, lost and gone forever. But the bushman in the queue uses every second and all his senses to be alert to whatever opportunities present themselves. If nothing else, it passes the time. And he knows that every queue has its moment, just like the airport queue, when you can push in without being seen as a cheat.

The best chance presents itself at what I call the 'brace'; it's that moment when the queue tenses as it starts to move – perhaps the checkout has just been manned or the barriers have been opened. Everyone squeezes closer and cranes to see what's happening. This is the moment to pounce. Everyone's far too busy guarding their space to notice, and the brace has broken any social bonds forged between neighbours in the line.

Know your queue

The queue you can never jump is the 'who's next?' queue. Here, there's no line, just a tacit agreement based on our incredible ability to remember the order of people who came after us. I've encountered this most recently waiting in a taxi office, but it's common in all kinds of waiting rooms, shops and offices. Without a word, everyone understands their role: to remember who has come after them. By a process of deduction, when only these stragglers are left, you know you're next. It's genius. And it can't be cracked.

The system at the bar in the pub is a version of this, when everyone knows who's next. But there's an added element of competition to see who can trick the barman into serving them before their turn. It's pushing in by mutual consent, where skill at getting served is more valued than time spent waiting.

DOS AND DON'TS AT THE BAR

The urban bushman can override years of experience in the saloon lounge with this back-of-a beer-mat guide:

- Put a hand on the bar, even if it has to snake through a crowd to get there.
- Eye contact with bar staff is crucial; they'll remember you if you smile.

- Point to someone at the bar to signal they're next. You'll be served after them.
- No coin tapping or note waving, it's just annoying.
- No shouting out or complaining. Bar staff are well practised at ignoring people like you.

THE OPTIMISTIC QUEUE

My favourite psychological test for showing the complexity of queue behaviour is the one performed on people waiting for a limited number of tickets, where the whole queue is asked what chance they think they have of getting one. For instance, in one queue for 140 tickets, questioners asked every 10th person in line how many people they thought were ahead of them. The first few were fairly accurate. Then, after 30 people or so, queuers started to overestimate the numbers in front. That went on until about 130, just where the ticket allocation would start to run out. Here people suddenly became more optimistic and started to underestimate the numbers ahead of them.

The same test has been done several times with the same result; people near the back consistently overestimate their chances, and inflated optimism starts to be shown at around the exact point where the cut-off will fall. One theory says that these people would have to be among life's optimists to have joined the queue so far back in the first place.

QUEUE THE DISNEY WAY

Disney theme park teams are experts at making people happy to queue for the big rides. They put up signs giving wait times that are purposely overestimated by 10 minutes or so. That way, when a 40-minute wait ends, people feel pleased they didn't have the anticipated 50-minute wait. Try it on the family next time they ask how long it'll be till you get there.

CASHPOINT TRACKING

If you ever stop to think about it (and believe me, I do), it's hard to fathom the logic of where cashpoints are sited. There just don't seem to be any hard-and-fast rules. The answer is to stop thinking and trust your urban instinct. Experience teaches you where to expect a cash machine. You can't explain what you're looking for, but you recognise the right conditions when you see them. Your brain has processed the information and drawn up a profile; it just doesn't bother you with the details. The best you can come up with is vague-seeming statements like, 'this looks like the right kind of street.' But don't be put off: trust your brain, because it's right.

As far as I can see, the profile assimilated by your unconscious over years of looking for a cashpoint is exactly the same as the one the banks use. You know what looks like the right kind of street but you just haven't felt the need to rationalise it. The banks do of course, and the result is the same.

It all comes down to safety. Not the safety of customers, but the safety of the men who put the money in. You see, banks don't want the cashpoint to be raided, or the men who fill them to be held up at gunpoint. So they stick to areas that fit the profile. And tell me these features aren't the same as those in your mind, if you really can:

- low-crime areas
- no areas of concealment where assailants might hide
- well lit
- monitored by CCTV
- good access for vehicles

If an area fits those criteria, it's a cashpoint zone, and where you find one machine, there are prabably others. By the way, I'm not talking about the cash machines that you find in corner shops that look more like a novelty money box. The criteria for those are the opposite of the above.

Urban bushcraft through the ages: Richard Ballantine

At first I thought it sounded like a book for kids ... *Richard's Bicycle Book*. I was 15 and wanted a serious manual where gear ratios, cadence and cable torque were discussed frankly and in full. I got all of that, and much more, as will become clear.

Richard is a bike guru, an evangelist of all things pedal-powered. A distaste for cars and their drivers oozes onto every page; so far, so standard. But one thing in the book etched an image onto my impressionable mind that's stayed with me ever since. This passage was expunged from later editions and every year or so I have to go back to my well-thumbed copy to make sure it was really there.

It's in the section about dogs and their habit of chasing bikes. Richard says that nine dogs out of ten are just trying to be friendly. But then he comes to the one that isn't. And in less than a page it turns into a bloodbath. The instructions on the various ways to kill a dog start with Richard describing swinging it round by the legs and dashing its brains out. But that's for a small dog. The big dog is next, and this is the bit few readers ever forget. With a single stroke of Richard's pen the innocent seeming bike pump becomes an instrument of death as your ram it down the gaping throat of the approaching dog. And if you haven't got a pump, says Richard, use your arm (up to your elbow). 'Better your arm than your throat,' he adds.

He obviously knows this is fairly intense. 'I have been advised what I have to say next is offensive. I do not think so,' he warns. Richard is committed to the cyclist's cause and wants no lily-livered squeamishness to stand in the way of completeness here. He wants to see menacing dogs despatched and the cyclist back on his bike. If that takes killing a dog, so be it. Now I sincerely hope no cyclist has ever had to put his pump to such grisly use, I really do. But for this lesson in improvisation, made all the more memorable by its shock value, Richard deserves his place among the greats.

THE PAVEMENT TANGO

Two people approach on the pavement and try to get out of each other's way, but instead they enter into a strange dance, each one mirroring the other, shuffling left and right, making it impossible to pass. This familiar and uncomfortable phenomenon is the face-off that was joyfully designated 'a droitwich'* by authors Douglas Adams and John Lloyd. It's the pedestrian equivalent of a stammer. A few people have tried to find a way to break the cycle but, until now, I haven't read one who has got it right.

First of all, forget any suggestion that on the pavement we obey a highway code, driving on the left or right depending on the law of the land. If that were true, the droitwich would never happen. The pedestrian in the right (that's on the left in the UK) would simply stick to their guns, just as in most traffic collisions.

On the pavement, we plan passing moves way ahead. Decisions are based on an advanced negotiation as each party makes tiny shows of intention, beamed along the pavement. We're so used to all this that we barely think about it. This is why a droitwich commonly occurs when you turn a corner – there's been no chance for the negotiation to take place.

But there are other forces at work here too, and gender plays a major role, with men tending to take the side nearest the road, and women preferring the inside lane. It's as if the man shields the woman from the traffic. Some see it as a relic of a more chivalrous age; I'm less sure, but nevertheless, it's true.

But because we're all in a hurry, we climb down very quickly if somebody signals the intention clearly to take the manlier path, whatever their sex. Normally these things are sorted out in an instant. The problem comes when two men make their move at the same moment. Both would rather avoid a face-off so both make the concession and step inside, and the droitwich is complete.

* *The Meaning of Liff*, by Douglas Adams and John Lloyd.

The Arndale heritage tour

It was 1959 when a pair of Leeds-based speculators called Arnold Hagenbach and Sam Chippindale had their vision of the future; modern shopping malls in brutalist concrete. But even before they'd built a single one, they added to our urban heritage when they bolted together bits of each of their names to form the magical word . . . Arn-dale.

Ahh, the Arndale! For all of us whose lives it touched, this one word summons up memories of shopping-centre life. It was Britain's introduction to American-style malls, and urban man had never seen the like. These concrete confections brought some sophistication to the neglected bits of the inner city, and the empire stretched from Luton to Accrington and Aberdeen to Eastbourne.

They staged car shows and beauty contests, and going 'down the Arndale' became quite the thing; this was a retail destination and generations of us were initiated in shopping-mall culture amid the graffiti and greeting card shops. As Arndale hit Australia it seemed the world had seen the future; and it was a concrete shopping mall. But then the bubble burst. The glitz of glass and chrome took over from concrete. The big brands moved to the new out-of-town super malls, and pound shops took their place.

Councils watched as the former retail showpiece became just a place to smoke a fag out of the rain. In desperate times they resorted to desperate measures, and nearly half of our Arndales were give chocolate-boxy new names. In Wellingborough the Arndale became Swansgate and in Bolton it's now Crompton Place, if you please. But these heritage sites have a significance that can't be erased; each one is a concrete milestone of our urban evolution. Next time you're near an Arndale, drop in and relive the magic. And if you fancy making the 22-stop tour, here's the itinerary in full: Aberdeen, Accrington, Bolton, Bradford, Doncaster, Eastbourne, Jarrow, Lancaster, Leeds (Armley), Leeds (Cross Gates), Leeds (Headingley), Luton, Manchester, Middleton, Morecambe, Nelson, Poole, Shipley, Sunderland, Stretford, Wandsworth, Wellingborough.

What's really happening is a bit like being sucked into a vortex, as conflicting forces collide: manners and convention, impatience and embarrassment, learned behaviour and instinct. And rather than solve it I prefer to celebrate this glorious revelation of the wonderful complexity at work in everyday actions.

NUT JITSU

People who walk around the city centre at night shouting abuse and threatening to punch people's lights out may tell you they're afraid of nothing. But it's not true. We are all afraid of loonies. I really don't mean mental illness in any clinical sense here; I mean the concept that we had in the playground of a proper nutter. Someone who starts spouting gibberish just makes us feel uneasy. A very high proportion of us would simply rather not be around them.

This rather ungenerous trait is worth remembering if you're ever unfortunate enough to be physically threatened by a stroppy stranger. Don't answer any of the inevitable questions ('You looking at me?' etc.). He knows what you're going to say, because he's heard all the rational answers before. Say something he's never heard before. Engage him, clearly and brightly, with irrelevant nonsense dug up from your childhood, or the last story you read the kids at bedtime. Just be normal, but talk nonsense. It should seem as if there's a burning issue that perhaps he can help you with: the mystery of the purple clouds, whether the taxis are giant beetles, anything like that. It should confuse things long enough for him to forget exactly why he wanted to punch you in the first place. And you'll probably settle for that.

Urban bushcraft through the ages:
Horace de Vere Cole

Here's a man who made it his life's work to turn the urban environment into his own personal playground. And what better way to end the urban bushman's city-centre adventure.

Horace de Vere Cole was Britain's greatest ever prankster. He was an Etonian aristocrat and the life and soul of the Bloomsbury set. But he's included here not for what he did but for the way he thought.

I sometimes wish old Horace had been less successful as a hoaxster. Then perhaps he'd have pointed his incredible energy in more useful directions. It's nice to know about his little stunts; how he invited people to a party only for them to discover as they were announced that all of their names ended in '-bottom', or how he'd walk around with bits from a cow's udder protruding from his fly, snipping it off with a wince once someone noticed it. But all this is just a frustrating glimpse of the double dose of confidence and exuberance coursing through his veins. With resources like that he'd have made a model urban bushman.

Look at his most famous tricks. There was the Dreadnought Hoax of 1910 when he conned the Royal Navy into welcoming him aboard its prized ship by posing as a visiting potentate from Abyssinia; or the time he directed a group of workmen to dig a hole in the middle of a central London street (the police even spent a day redirecting traffic around the hole before anyone asked questions). Each one shows planning, poise and precision. He knew how fallible all humans really are, and was endlessly amused by the chance to prove it. But he could only pull his hoaxes off because he put his sense of fun before all fear and doubt.

My favourite is the theatre date for baldies. He handed out free tickets to as many bald men as he could, who all duly took their seats as directed. Then, at the interval, his plan came to fruition as the lights came up to reveal a jolly rude word spelled out in bald pates. It's reported that he did such a perfect job that there was even a dot over the 'i'.

Horace must have been irritating as hell to have around, but from the safe distance of a hundred years he's a godsend, and a great example to all urban bushmen. Rules, conventions and manners only inspired greater expressions of his individuality through meticulous expositions of the simplicity of all human life.

5.
WHEN DISASTER STRIKES

The urban bushman doesn't deal in the kind of emergency that you may see described elsewhere; you know the kind of thing, the collapse of civilisation, global apocalypse and all that stuff. It's just not his main concern. What bothers him much more are the disasters he confronts from day to day; the broken coffee machine, no firelighters for the barbecue, and having to carry a load of washing to the launderette when the bag isn't big enough. What he wants are real solutions for real crises.

The following starter kit will help you reach a state of total readiness from which you can build up your own repertoire of techniques, and prepare for all eventualities (barring global disaster* of course).

* In the unlikely event that you find yourself in a post-apocalyptic survival scenario, here's what you do: locate a survivor wearing belted shorts and a smug grin (he'll probably be weaving fish traps or building a canoe from the bark of a tree). Now ask for a light. He'll be so keen to demonstrate his ability to spark up an ember that you'll have just enough time to swipe his gear. No need to feel guilty: after all, he was the one who wanted to live by his wits.

9-VOLT BATTERY   **'BRILLO' SCOURER**   **TOILET ROLL**

THE URBAN FIRELIGHTING KIT

Forget firelighters and a big box of matches; all you need for effortless fire lighting every time (and always in a controlled non-flammable environment) is a wire scouring pad (or some wire wool) and a battery. The 9-volt battery is the kind that goes into radios and it's best for the job simply because the terminals are both on the same end. Toilet paper is the standard item to use as tinder, but anything that burns quickly and easily will do.

Hold the Brillo Pad loosely at one end and dab the other end onto the terminals. It will start to glow and fizz immediately. Just touch a few sheets of loo roll onto it and blow to encourage the flames.

Despite the similarity in appearance, this doesn't work with Shredded Wheat.

How it works

As soon as the wire touches the terminals it makes a circuit. Electricity flows through the tiny strands of wire wool, making them so hot that they glow red and start to burn. It's the same principle as Edison's ingenious light bulb, as demonstrated by him in 1879. He used a tungsten filament, and put it in a vacuum so it couldn't burn, but only glow.

This does drain power from the battery. A 9-volt battery can light a few fires but on a week-long camping trip be prepared to get through a few of them.

NO WIRE WOOL? NO PROBLEM, USE A CAR BATTERY . . .

Holding them safely, attach some jump leads to the battery in the normal way and prepare a little ball of tinder. Put the tinder on the ground and quickly touch the terminals together with the tinder. The sparks will easily be enough to get a glowing ember or two, and with a few little puffs, a flame. Cotton wool, upholstery straw, the lint from inside an anorak or puffer jacket, belly button fluff, it will all do the job.

LIFE WITHOUT MATCHES

The friction match was invented in 1827. But for tens of thousands of years up to that point, fire lighting was a skill touched by magic and mystery. Flints and fire starters were cherished possessions. And most appealing of all, lighting fires was something men could be good at. So it's hardly surprising that, despite its new-found convenience, the fire-lighting ritual lost none of its man appeal, whether it was in the Western legend of cowboys striking matches on their stubble or using the rugged gas-guzzling Zippo lighter. Fire is man's greatest technological triumph and we're always going to have a weakness for staring into the flames.

It's summed up pretty well by Ellsworth Jaeger, an authority on Native American bushcraft, in his 1945 book, *Wildwood Wisdom*: '. . . whether we realize it or not all our ancestral memories come surging to the surface from the depths of our beings when we sit around the campfire. We too are stirred by its magic, even as were our shadowy ancestors long ago.' Absolutely, Ellsworth . . . now pass me a Brillo Pad.

FIRELIGHTING WITH A COKE CAN AND A CHOCOLATE BAR

This little secret is popular with kids, but it's still a *bona fide* grown-up technique. You could wait a long time for a genuine need to light a fire using the contents of a lunch box so grab the chance next time you've got an urge to experiment. The classic way into this is to present someone with the can and chocolate and challenge them to light a fire.

What you need are the following:

- fizzy drink can
- chocolate bar
- tinder (as mentioned earlier, the lint from inside a puffer jacket or anorak works well)
- sunshine

How it works

The sunshine gives it away. It's a version of the old Boy Scout trick where you use a magnifying glass to burn ants, but just a lot better. The secret ingredients are the can's concave bottom and the magical polishing properties of chocolate. Put them both together and you'll have a mirror that can focus the sun's rays into an intense spot of light able to get your tinder smoking in seconds.

Use little lumps of chocolate just like shoe polish on the bottom of the can, rubbing hard with the wrapper until it starts to shine. Work at it until it's so shiny you get crazy 'hall of mirrors' reflections in the can. It will take half an hour or so, but you'll get there – it's all to do with the slightly abrasive properties of choc. Any type of chocolate will do, the purer the better.

DO NOT eat the chocolate after use! It picks up aluminium from the can, which is toxic.

Now that the lens is ready you need to find the focal point. One good way is to use a scrap of newspaper that's white on one side and heavily printed on the other. Point the can at the sun and hold the paper so that the white side is towards the can. On the black side you should see a spot of light. Move the paper closer and further away from the can to find the point where the spot is smallest. That's the focal point, as you'll see when the paper starts to smoulder.

Screw up the chocolate wrapper and put it in the middle of a nest of tinder: twigs, leaves or anything that will burn. Focus the beam on your tinder, and as soon as it starts to smoke encourage it to flame by gently blowing on it.

If you're doing everything right, it should take five seconds or so until the wrapper's setting fire to your nest of tinder.

If the polishing takes too long with chocolate and you think you can live with yourself afterwards there are other quicker options. But beware, there's a law of diminishing returns: as the polishing agent becomes more effective the primal job satisfaction is diminished. It becomes less bushcraft, more DIY.

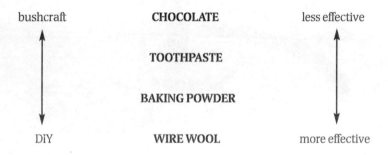

	CHOCOLATE	
bushcraft		less effective
	TOOTHPASTE	
	BAKING POWDER	
DIY	**WIRE WOOL**	more effective

HOW TO MAKE YOUR TROUSERS INTO A RUCKSACK

You pop into a supermarket to get a pint of milk, then you pick up a few other things until you've got both arms full and a cereal box under your chin. It doesn't only happen in the supermarket either. Sometimes there's just too much to carry. Here's a solution that'll keep your hands free when you've got an unexpected load.

The trouser pack is an old hobo classic that you'd have used if you were riding the boxcars in 1930s' America. But there's a lot of life in it yet, and once you've mastered the knack you'll find plenty of opportunity to use it. The supreme function for the trouser pack is transporting a bundle of dirty clothes to the launderette, but it's good for family trips to the beach too. It's obviously best when there's an extra pair of trousers around so that you don't leave yourself with cold knees.

You need:

- one pair of trousers
- belt or similar length rope
- two lengths of rope/cord (15in or so)

Use the belt/rope as a drawstring to pull through the belt hoops. Bundle up your goods into the top of the trousers and close tightly with the drawstring. Now place the bag with the opening downwards onto your back, so that the legs can come over your shoulders.

Stuff the trouser ends into the belt loop and wind them around again. This will hold firm but also allow you to make adjustments.

Having the trousers upside down allows you to have the wider more comfortable part of the leg over your shoulder, but as an alternative you can have the legs coming up from under your armpits and over the top. The great benefit of this is the accessible back pockets, though it's at the expense of a slightly less generous shoulder strap.

EMERGENCY COFFEE DEVICE

Every coffee taster knows that the best coffee is made by the filter method. And we all know that just because it's an emergency there's no need to compromise on standards (Galton's Code, see p. 63).

In a crisis, when gourmet coffee is called for, here's how a large plastic bottle comes to the rescue.

You need:

- large plastic bottle, clean
- knife/sharp scissors
- filter papers

1. Put the kettle on.

2. Slice the bottle somewhere below the neck, preferably at the widest part, to make a funnel. Keep in mind that the 'bottom' is the main coffee receptacle, so don't make it too small.

3. Place the funnel in the bottom part. If it slips through, slightly twist it so that it jams in place.

4. Put your filter paper into the funnel and add coffee.

5. After the water's boiled, let it stop bubbling and gently pour the required amount onto the coffee.

THE BROADSHEET BODY WARMER

Think of people using newspapers to keep warm and you think of tramps on park benches. But this convenient emergency body warmer wasn't always so down at heel, and now it's time to put it back where it belongs. It's a socially mobile system that's a blessing wherever you might be . . . waiting for a bus, sitting at a football match or waiting outside the palace to receive an honour.

Stuffing a paper up your jumper to keep warm is a piece of urban lore that began with the well-off middle classes when caught out by a cold snap while at the races or out riding. I found references to it in two newspapers from the turn of the last century when gentlemen are advised: 'an excellent chest protector for a cold day is a folded newspaper buttoned under the overcoat.'

Cycle couriers have been using this trick for years; a newspaper down the front to keep out the wind chill and one at the back for extra insulation. For full coverage, a larger-format newspaper or old-fashioned broadsheet is preferred.

In cases of extreme cold you can make a really big difference by inserting a snug filling of scrunched-up newspaper between the main newspaper and your body or undergarments. Fill in around the entire torso, front and back, to keep your vital organs warm.

BREAK A LOCK WITH A SOCK

Cheap combination locks . . . you know they aren't a good idea when you buy them, but somehow they draw you in with that seductive offer of instant personalisation; use any combination you like, a set of three numbers you'll always remember. Now, what was it again . . .?

Breaking a lock apart with a sock when you've forgotten the code is not only a handy way to open it, but also a pretty powerful demonstration of why you should never buy such a lock again.

Here's what to do:
- Remove one sock.
- Slip it through the horseshoe-shaped part of the lock.
- Grab one end of the sock in each hand and give both a sharp tug, away from the lock barrel.
- Try it three of four times.

This is a last-ditch attempt to open a troublesome lock. If it works then the satisfaction may go some way towards countering the shame you're now feeling at having a lock that can be broken into with a sock!

If you want a less brutal way into your lock, try cracking the combination; it's normally pretty easy on a cheap lock.

Pull up the horseshoe bar as far as it will go and turn each number wheel until you feel a small click on the bar, or until the wheel is harder to turn. It's as simple as that.

This hardly turns you into Raffles the gentleman jewel thief, but it feels good all the same.

THE URBAN ROBINSON CRUSOE TEST
SIXTY MINUTES ON A TRAFFIC ISLAND

In the first few days of his 20 years marooned on a desert island, Robinson Crusoe had to choose what to salvage from the wreck of his ship. He started with rum and tobacco, but then got a bit more practical and hauled back all kinds of useful odds and ends. It's a scenario that's often mimicked on survival courses, where students get a minute to pick the five or ten items they'd salvage from a ship or plane crash.

Well here's the urban bushcraft version. Based on what you've learned through this section of the book, could you pick what you need when the pressure's really on?

Here's the scenario. You've run out of petrol by the roadside and there's an hour to wait till the breakdown man gets through the traffic. What would you buy at the corner shop for under a fiver? All items must serve genuine survival priorities – fire, shelter, warmth etc.

Here's one exemplary set of purchases offering options for fire lighting, warmth, sustenance and a chance to catch up on the price of your shares or the racing results.

Bar of chocolate	50p
Fizzy drink	80p
Toilet roll (× 2)	60p
Newspapers (x 3)	£1.90
Brillo Pads (× 10)	£1.00
--	
TOTAL	£4.80

Urban bushcraft through the ages:
Edward Barton-Wright

If urban bushcraft is all about updating and adapting traditional survival skills for the modern city then E.W. Barton-Wright is absolutely one of us. He's a man who might have been remembered for his moustache alone, but Edward Barton-Wright is commemorated here as the inventor of the urban martial art of Bartitsu, self-defence with a walking-stick or umbrella (he also had techniques for repelling attack using a hat, coat and that new-fangled contraption, the bicycle).

After studying ju-jitsu in Japan, B.-W. returned to London in 1898 to find a violent and fearful city. Ruffians lurked in dim, gas-lit alleys and the newspapers were full of fearful stories of garrotters and muggers, picking off their victims from among the new middle classes. So B.-W. turned his energies to devising a thoroughly modern martial art for the new industrial city.

These modern criminals flouted the old rules of fair play and refused to fight by the established rules. Bartitsu offered the chance for a gentleman to retain his dignity while ensuring he was more than a match for any assailant under these 'unequal conditions'.

These days there's a rough form of no-holds-barred combat called Ultimate Fighting. Bartitsu was its Edwardian antecedent. It blended ju-jitsu with kickboxing and stick fighting, and it meant business. Launching Bartitsu in a popular periodical* in 1898, B.-W. wrote: 'blows can be made so formidable that with an ordinary cane it is possible to sever a man's jugular vein through the collar of his overcoat.'Techniques were devised for a parade of unfortunate scenarios involving assailants with sticks and staffs, in crowds and in one-to-one combat. Practitioners were taught how to bayonet their attacker in the solar plexus with a walking-stick, how to use the crook of an umbrella to pull 'a ruffian' off his feet, and how to distract an attacker by shrouding him with an unbuttoned overcoat.

And even though decades have passed, the sequence of photographs illustrating each move shows the balletic poise with which Barton-Wright swept aside his opponents, and of which he was rightly proud.

Barton-Wright was a man after my own heart, equipping his students for the new and very real challenges of life in a modern city. Until then, men had felt protected by the rules of decency and fair play, but that old order had crumbled. Bartitsu helped the modern gentleman meet this new test with pragmatism and dignity. Hoorah for B.-W.

* *Pearson's Magazine*, a highbrow version of today's *Esquire* and, incidentally, the first periodical to carry a crossword.

6.
WORKPLACE STRATEGY

At work we operate under strict rules about what to say, what to do and when to go home. And whether it's the glint of your cufflinks or the cut of your jeans, the way you look matters too. Work is now the most formal event in our lives. And it's under constraints like these that our primal urges long to rebel, and to show themselves in all their glory.

Ever since childhood we've learned to obey rules that go against instinct: we put the toilet seat down, use a knife and fork impeccably, and hardly ever spill custard down our front. So by now we're pretty good at hiding the urges within. Sitting in a meeting, suited and booted, shaved and deodorised, we play the game of pretending that this is all there is, that our animal appetites are sated with the new business plans, that our life's aim is to see the merger proposal accepted by head office. And subsequently everyone around the table keeps their primal self buttoned up and reined in. It's there alright and we know it. It's reliably uncouth, totally unprofessional and never to be mentioned. It's the woolly mammoth in the room.

But the urban bushman refuses to make his inner caveman redundant, preferring to recruit him as a trusty ally to help in the fight against drudgery at a desk, or boredom in the budget hotel. Whether flicking rubber bands across the office or swapping glances in the meeting room he knows this is where his instincts can reap dividends. By embracing his savage side the bushman at work can let off steam, make the days fly by, and, when needs must, even get a bit more work done.

IN A MEETING

'I'm sorry I can't talk now, I'm in a meeting . . .'

The business meeting is a fenced-off piece of formality, a ritual that's entirely sacrosanct. Here are a few tips to help the bushman emerge from the meeting room unscathed.

Once upon a time turning up without a tie and calling your boss by his first name would have got you the sack. Now it's just the way work is. But don't be deceived. All this apparent informality on the surface doesn't change what goes on beneath it. It's a battle for status, power and personal gain – in a nutshell, all of the stuff that's worth getting out of bed for.

TIMING IS EVERYTHING

The most powerful person in the meeting is the last one to walk in before it starts. The message is that things can only happen once they're in the room. This is when being late is a privilege of power. The lowest-status person is the one who arrives after it starts. This is an open statement that their role is unimportant. They were just plain late.

The village elders of Madagascar and Sir Alan Sugar know all about the privilege of being late. They know how to time their entrance into a meeting. Just like 'Sir Alan' in *The Apprentice* they want to be the last to walk into the room. It shows they hold the power. But in the village there's a problem. There are a lot of elders and they all want to be the last to arrive. So they've developed a system whereby instead of arriving late, the meeting is announced two hours early. The villagers arrive on time, then eventually the elders show up with the appropriate delay. And finally the chief arrives latest of all and things can start.

STAY STANDING; THE HANNIBAL LECTER TRICK

Have we all seen *The Silence of the Lambs*? Well, you know that bit when Jodie Foster as the FBI agent first meets Anthony Hopkins as the scary cannibal? The camera follows as she walks into the dingy prison wing and along a corridor towards his cell. Then the music builds, and we're seeing her point of view, and we know we're about to meet a killer. What happens next is chilling. As he's revealed to us for the first time, Dr Hannibal Lecter isn't sitting in a corner or lying on his bed, but standing to attention in the middle of his cell, staring straight at her. He knew she was coming, and he's waiting for her. It's the start of a police interview where the criminal is the one who does the questioning. He's the one who's locked up, yet he seems to hold all the cards. And it all starts with him standing up.

I often think about this when I'm in a meeting room being made to wait. Sitting down is a passive submission to a timetable imposed by somebody else. All you can do is wait for them to show up so that things can start. It gives them all of the power. Try staying standing until they arrive, and make them sit first. Things will start when you choose to sit. That way you keep the initiative and, like Hannibal Lecter, take control.

THE POWER OF SILENCE

This is an old classic of the antiques' trader and second-hand car dealer – i.e. urban tribespeople with an innate expertise in bargaining hard, standing firm and making the other guy crumble. The golden rule is to say to yourself: 'The next one to speak, loses.' Then shut up and prove yourself right.

In the creative brainstorm session the bushman's colleagues yak on in the vain hope of hitting home with one incisive remark. In the meeting room the flip charts fly. Oversized pages are filled with meaningless phrases. If work is the home of bullshit, and it surely is, then the flip chart must be the toilet paper.

But while his colleagues clamour to fill every available silence with the sound of their voice the bushman remains aloof, watching from a distance. He sees that silence is the one thing that generates more drivel than anything else, and the thing that every office worker fears the most. So he keeps quiet and turns silence to his own advantage.

This works purely because silence is unnerving. To stay silent is to suggest an inner calm, and that's sure to unnerve any office opponent. The more confident you are in your silence the more churned up in self-doubt they'll become.

Here's how to use it. You're in a frank exchange of views with a colleague. You sense they aren't going to back down. They're convinced they are right. Now ask them a critical question, something related to their professional judgement. Listen to their answer and wait for them to stop. Then hold that eye contact and just say nothing. This is where they start to squirm. Your silence unnerves then so much they begin to babble, and then you've got them. They'll start to show you all the flaws in their argument, dredge up their doubt and indecision, and lay it before you. Anything but silence.

This is also an old favourite in negotiations. Instead of reacting to your counterpart's offer just say nothing. Pretty soon they'll fill the silence with a lower offer.

GO UNDERCOVER WITHOUT LEAVING YOUR DESK

Leaving your coat on the back of your chair when you slip off early, diverting your office phone to your mobile – there are all kinds of ways the bushman can cover his tracks at work. Here's how the email application on your desktop computer can provide virtual cover, just when you need it most.

I once got a circular email, sent to the whole company, asking if anyone had a large bird outfit. More specifically, it had to be a black or brown bird such as a crow or thrush, and definitely not a chicken, robin or duck. It was a change from the usual stuff about missing staplers, but it demonstrates the depth of a problem the urban bushman confronts every day. Our inboxes are clogged with trivialities. They arrive with a ping and a tempting envelope icon, and then slowly consume our time in little one-minute parcels. But all that changes when you learn to use your inbox to go undercover.

Before email, when people picked up the phone, secretaries and receptionists had to lie and to cover their boss's tracks by making excuses and saying he was out. But now the threat comes by email and there's no secretary to deflect them. There's a simple solution, however, in this democratic world of new technology. Just switch on the Out of Office assistant.

Think about it. When you send an email and get back an Out of Office message, who suspects for a moment it might not be true? Who wonders whether this is just a cover story – a cunning ploy allowing us to work on something more worthwhile than responding to email? Nobody does, because we believe what our computer tells us. The Out of Office function is the best liar in the office. It would be stupid not to use it.

OFFICE SPYCRAFT: PASSWORD HACKING

Password protecting your email inbox is a fundamental rule of office life, so the bushman can't resist the challenge of working out the password of everyone in the office. Not because he wants to get into their inbox and send obscene messages to the MD; of course not! This classic piece of spycraft is dignified with a far more gentlemanly outcome.

1. Pick your target and begin observation. You need to be standing near them as they log in. Pick out single letters and numbers as they type, one or two per day. Start at the very beginning or the very end of the password sequence. This is easier for touch typists, but we all have a fairly good understanding of what's where on the keyboard.

2. Log your observations, noting if you can where each keystroke comes in the order.

3. Listen to the rhythm and tap it out on a keyboard, counting the number of keystrokes made. Once your list has nearly enough characters, start trying to crack the code. Think of it as an anagram and find a likely word, such as the name of your target's child, home town or pet.

Try out the options on another computer (one which allows you to log in twice) or on your target's computer when they're not around. It shouldn't take long before you crack it. Well done! Now you have the password, here's what to do. It just wouldn't be right not to inform your colleague that their secret is out. Design a calling card and leave it on their desk to let them know they've been anonymously hacked. This gives the whole exercise a spot of class worthy of the gentleman jewel thief Raffles. But it also gives you the upper hand. Though you didn't read any of their private files, they aren't to know that, and there can be nothing more unnerving.

Set yourself the target of cracking the target password within two weeks, or ten days, of observation. Canadian spy instructors who worked on this system reckon on needing nine days to crack a password.

PASSWORDS FOR PLEBS

Two recent surveys, one in America and one in Britain, show that the thought process leading to an easy-to-hack password is startlingly similar – no matter which side of the Atlantic you're on. And, apparently, true simpletons everywhere have a curious attraction to typing the word 'monkey'.

AMERICA'S MOST POPULAR PASSWORDS	BRITAIN'S MOST POPULAR PASSWORDS
password	123
123456	password
qwerty	Liverpool
abc123	letmein
letmein	123456
monkey	qwerty
myspace1	Charlie
password1	monkey
Blink182	Arsenal
10. (Your first name)	Thomas

Football team loyalty is a stronger strand in the UK than in the USA. But in this particular league table, having a simple one-word name seems to be a particular advantage. Well-supported teams like Manchester United and Newcastle United lose out to the likes of Liverpool and Arsenal.

Any password used in a TV series is always popular. When agent Fox Mulder in *The X-Files* revealed his, it surged up the polls. It was trustno1.

OFFICE WARFARE

To some it's a juvenile distraction; to others it's a way to give the warrior inside a workout without having to join your colleagues sweating their lunch hour away in a kick-boxing class.

Ever since he first slung a jacket on the back of his swivel chair and played around with the lever under the seat, working man has been looking for a way to relax at work. If only he could quickly tune out and rediscover what life's all about, then he'd get back to the sales figures like never before.

From fag break to screen break he's tried a number of different things. Stress balls and executive toys worked for a while but too much staring at a Newton's Cradle can lead into some dark and dangerous places. Then came team-building breaks and water-cooler moments, but getting cosy and communal with his colleagues wasn't really what he had in mind.

But by using the resources of the office environment to revive man's primal purpose, urban bushcraft has hit on the perfect formula for a happy workforce. With nothing but a few office booby traps and a pocket full of rubber bands, he's perfectly equipped to get through te 9–5 with a spring in his step and without a knife in his back.

STEALTH GUN WITH A HIGHLIGHTER PEN

The slippery top of those fat office highlighter pens allows a unique opportunity to fire, seemingly by accident. As illustrated on the previous page, all you need is a pen and strong document clip (bulldog clip). Here's how to do it:

- Take the lid off the highlighter and squeeze the sides together a bit. Now fix the clip to the lid, slightly off-centre.
- Lightly put the lid back on the pen, but don't push it down.
- Adopt an innocent and uncaring expression, and hold it.
- When you're ready to fire, point the clip handles towards the target and press the lid down firmly onto the pen. The slight flexibility of the lid means it will expand, forcing the clip to fly off in your chosen direction. You, of course, will appear oblivious.

RUBBER BANDS: SOME ADVANCED AERODYNAMICS

When an office bushman worthy of the name spends his career near a stationery cupboard stocked with boxes of rubber bands, the result is something truly extraordinary.

Flicking rubber bands off the end of your thumb is fine for the classroom, but with this technique, rubber-band aerodynamics rises to the level of the boardroom.

With a simple adjustment to firing technique the rubber band is turned from a uselessly floppy projectile into an aerodynamic miracle with swerve, lift and a rather marvellous swooshing sound as it strafes your colleague's ear.

THE TECHNIQUE

A large rubber band is all you need.

1. Hook the band over the index finger of your lead hand (for me it's the left) and pull it back by hooking it with the middle finger of your rear hand (my right).

2. When it's stretched fairly tight put your thumb up through the hoop and pull the band back further still with your thumb instead of the finger which you now need to take out of the way. This switch pulls the band in a different direction, slightly to one side. That's what's meant to happen. One side of the band (the left) is now much tighter than the other.

3. Hold steady and take aim by lining up your thumb and the front finger, like the sights of a gun. The band will fly in a curve to the right (away from the tighter side), so aim to the left of the target.

4. Fire by gently lowering the thumb and watch your band swerve as it flies. Listen for that swoosh. Once your colleagues get to know that sound it will strike fear in their heart, earning you their undying respect and giving you the edge in any skirmish.

Now practise and practise some more. Pretty soon you'll be able to predict and adjust the swerve, and hit targets round corners.

How it works

The secret of this technique is in the lop-sided pull back, making one side stretch more than the other, so that on release it spins in flight. The spinning band forms a flat disk with uncanny aerodynamic properties. It has a curved path that's predictable enough to allow for extreme accuracy, and the extra lift produces a flight with 50–70 per cent more range than a standard flick.

Plausible deniability

One of many great things about curved flight is that the band hits its target from a direction that rules you out as a suspect. And as there's no gun or launcher, there's no evidence to pin it on you. You have plausible deniability.

RUBBER BANDS – A REFRESHER

In the event of office warfare you may need a refresher on the correct way to fire a rubber band. It's been a few years since school, after all. As all schoolboys know, there are one- and two-handed techniques, both imitating a gun to allow you to roam the office firing at will.

THE HANDGUN

- Load the band by wrapping it around the tip of the little finger, which is curled towards the base of the thumb.
- Stretch the other end of the band behind the thumb and hook it over the extended index finger. Your handgun is now loaded.
- To fire, gently release the little finger.

This is especially suitable for the short thicker rubber bands, used to tie bundles of asparagus.

THE SEMI-AUTOMATIC

Here the band is held by the vertical thumb of the front hand while the other end is gripped between thumb and first finger of the rear 'trigger' hand, which pulls back for maximum tension before releasing. This is more suitable for a longer rubber band.

THE OFFICE TRAPPER

Lying in wait for a victim to blunder into our trap is a pleasure that runs deep in our DNA, from the Sumatran pig hunter setting his pitfall trap to the schoolboy balancing a cup of water over the classroom door. And the workplace is the ideal environment to reconnect with the trapper within.

For primitive man, traps saved on hours of running around with a spear and allowed him a rare sit-down. Hunting like this had it all: there was the careful construction, the tense anticipation, and then the eventual satisfaction of a job well done. But best of all, trapping made him feel clever. It's a game of chess we've been playing for thousands of years, against some pretty dumb opponents, and not surprisingly we've grown to like it.

In the old days, trap design was passed down from father to son, over generations. Now things move a bit faster, and they're passed around in seconds over the internet. Given that half the planet seems to work in an office, there's a rich culture to draw on, and you've got every chance of finding the ideal trap for the particular challenges of your office.

Plentiful free materials and lots of spare time make for perfect conditions in which to develop your skills as a virtuoso of desktop defence gadgets. This one is fiddly to make, but the principle is simple enough. Make your own modifications as you go along, and if it works, go with it.

The builders and designers of OfficeGuns.com and Instructables.com are working hard to keep office weaponry and trapping alive. I'm grateful to them for their inspiration and for showing me I'm not alone.

A NOTE ON PREY

Usually, in the average workplace, there's no shortage of victims to choose from. This is a place where squabbles over territory escalate into open war, where persistent offences like stealing a newspaper from your desk or hogging the photocopier can fuel a ravenous hunger for revenge.

But choose your prey carefully. The wise bushman prefers to rise above everyday quarrels, preferring to not give away his presence by targeting obvious rivals. Instead he moves around unseen, picking the most demanding of challenges in the knowledge that, to the hunter, the real thrill is always in the chase.

THE HOT DESK MOUSE TRAP

When sharing desks gets too much don't lock your computer; booby trap it.

This is a pretty simple device to get you going, powered by a domestic mouse trap, and sprung by any tiny movement on the computer mouse. It's designed to encourage the colleague using your desk to find an alternative place to spend a few hours on Facebook.

Once the trap is set, as soon as your colleague moves that mouse a shower of your choice* rains down on a wide area within a metre or so of the monitor. The great thing about it is that the trigger mechanism can stay completely out of sight.

What you need:
- Coat hanger
- Mouse trap

* A small amount of water (from the cooler, of course) works well, if you're prepared for the desk to get wet. Otherwise a pot of glitter gets the message across, with the added benefit of wider 'footprint'.

- A film canister or cup (if firing water)
- Gaffer tape (duct tape)
- Pliers
- Fishing line
- Water/glitter

What to do:

- First, find a level platform behind your monitor where you can fix the trap.
- Now use the wire from the coat hanger to extend the arms of the mousetrap to reach over the top of the monitor. This has the added benefit of giving your chosen projectile more velocity.
- Tape the film canister, paper cup or other small receptacle to the end of the new arm you've just made.
- Fix a length of fishing line to the trigger bit (where the mouse nibbles the cheese) so that any slight tug will spring the trap.
- Firmly secure with tape the whole assembly to the back of the monitor, or just behind it. It needs to be horizontal and on a steady base.
- Thread the length of wire or fishing line discreetly behind the monitor and attach it to the mouse cable, out of sight.
- Now set the trap (extremely carefully) and retreat. Oh, and as most people discover when they do this the first time, don't fill anything with water until the very end.

Warning: Range finding is a big issue with this trap, but that can be assessed on a trial run with just a few ripped shreds of paper in the canister.

As soon as the trap is sprung you make yourself a highly prized target for a similar trap. Trust me, I know from experience.

BIRO BOW AND ARROW

There's a time when every hunter has to give up trapping and stalk his prey instead. This biro bow and arrow is his weapon of choice.

Raid the stationery cupboard for a biro with a slightly flexible body and a rubber band that can just loop around it lengthways.

Take the pen to bits and use a small cross head (Phillips type) screwdriver, or anything spiked, to prod a hole in the middle. The hole must be just big enough to push the nib holder through. If you're using a hard plastic pen you'll struggle to get a hole through it without it shattering. Hook the rubber band around the pen body, insert your arrow, pull back, and take aim.

The best use for this potentially harmful weapon is in the controlled environment of an office shooting range. Most importantly of all, don't point or fire it towards anybody's face.

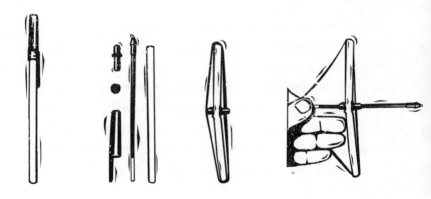

FIZZY SWEETS – THE EMERGENCY DEODORANT

ARMPIT CHEMISTRY FOR THE WORKPLACE

An underarm emergency can strike anytime. But it seems to happen more than anywhere else, at work. And then it is truly a crisis.

In corporate meeting rooms the safely synthetic whiff of marker pens and new carpet mingles happily with the overhead projector's top note of singed fluff. But there's no place at all for the animal smell of the adult human. In fact anyone suspected of bringing in a bit of body fug may as well start peeing in the corner to mark their territory.

But there's a neat pocket-sized solution whenever the deodorant's out of reach – a packet of fizzy sweets. Just slipping a crushed Love Heart under your armpit averts a crisis for you (and anyone sitting next to you), neutralising your body's odour in minutes. And as a reassuring extra, there's a little fizz of confirmation as this piece of armpit chemistry works its magic.

How it works

The important ingredient is bicarbonate of soda (also called baking soda); after sugar, it's the main ingredient of fizzy sweets, sherbet and the like. Bicarbonate of soda is a crystalline grain that's mildly alkaline, which neutralises the armpit's acidic scent molecules, to work as a deodoriser.

In sweets, the soda's job is to fizz when sucked, so it's still in an active state. In baked goods like scones and muffins the same ingredient has already done its work by making the mixture rise, so it's no longer fizzy.

TOP-THREE CONFECTIONARY DEODORANTS

- Sherbet Fountain (handy and reusable, keep one in your desk drawer)
- Love Hearts (5 to 10 sweets, crushed, per armpit)
- Swizzles (one packet per armpit)

Warning: Avoid Parma Violets and other strongly coloured sweets – they work well but the stains on your shirt will be a dead giveaway.

THE BOREDOM OF THE BUSINESS TRAVELLER

One thing and one thing alone can ease the tedium of the drab business hotel. When the walls start closing in, cooking on the built-in appliances is a tonic for the soul. Most of the stuff you need can be bought in the local shop or picked up for free around the hotel. Get the Do Not Disturb sign on the door, and start cooking.

THE HOTEL-ROOM CHEF

You're staying in a hotel designed for corporate travellers. The Carvery closed half an hour ago and a room service club sandwich is the price of dinner for two at your local takeaway. You could go out, of course, but that would mean mingling with your fellow delegates when all you really want to do is to take off your name badge and reclaim your feral identity. It's time to get cooking with your hotel-room appliances.

Look around the room; it's stuffed with gadgets, and every one of them can be turned into a cooker. I'm just going to start you off with a few of my old favourites; once your bushman brain gets into gear, I've no doubt you'll be inventing plenty more. After all, food is a great incentive.

Of course, all of these methods can be used elsewhere; it's just that I know how soul destroying these hotel bedrooms can be. Take care not to cause any damage, but don't worry about the mess, the maids have seen far worse.

THE HOTEL COOK'S TOOLKIT

Keep your cookery kit in a spare wash bag ready to drop into your luggage in a second. If you're going on a flight, check security and customs restrictions.

The kit comprises:

- Aluminium foil – several long sheets
- Wire strippers
- A small metal grill (optional)
- Instant noodles
- Shrink-wrapped hot dogs/pancakes/burritos
- Maple syrup

Once in the hotel take any chance to pocket sachets of condiments, seasoning, plastic knives etc. and borrow some cutlery from the dining room as soon as you check in. Don't feel bad, you've paid for it.

Cooking hot dogs by electrocution is a staple of American culture. In the 1960s it was a standard science experiment in school, and, at home, the Presto Hot Dogger was a familiar gadget. The whole family could watch as 120 volts passed through the writhing, steaming hot dogs accompanied by electric sizzling and the smell of burning flesh. 'Cooks 12 hot dogs in 60 seconds', boasted the TV ads.

THE 100-WATT HOT DOG

The plain old bedside lamp is a good place to start. Before long, by the magical properties of the discovery of Messrs Ohm, Faraday and Edison, you'll be tucking into the quickest hot dogs you've ever eaten.

What you need:

- A lamp or light fitting
- Wire cutters/blade
- Pre-packed hot dogs/bratwurst/frankfurters
- Ketchup/mustard and bread (optional)

Warning: If you can change a light bulb and wire a plug then you're probably qualified to carry out the electrical rewiring this job requires. Just be sure not to touch any bare wires or the 'live' hot dog when the plug is switched on.

What to do:

All you're doing really is plugging in your hot dog and allowing electricity to fry it from the inside. The American domestic current of 120 volts allows for a slower cooking time, which is better for flavour. But the European standard 240 volts breaks the record for speed.

There are two options for wiring up your hot dog. You can take the ends of the cable out of the lamp and use them as your cooking 'prongs', them just rewire the lamp after use. Or, if there's a lot of spare flex, you may get away with slightly adjusting it, by cutting it near the plug and once you've eaten simply rewiring the plug. Remember to remove the scrap piece of flex in case it arouses suspicion.

- Unplug lamp and switch off plug.
- Prepare a bare end of cable by stripping the plastic insulation from the two wires inside, to give you an exposed section that's just longer than your hot dog. Stick both wires lengthways into the hot dog sausage and wrap them together where they stick out of the other end.
- Now just plug in. Don't touch the sausage or wires!
- Switch on the power and allow 2–3 seconds to cook (in the UK and Europe at 220–240 volts).
- Unplug the lamp, remove your hot dog, place in bun and tuck in.

For a slower-cooked hot dog, strip just a few centimetres of each cable and put one into each end of the hot dog. This will take 2–3 minutes to cook through.

Cut out and leave any black or charred parts of the hot dog – they may contain nasty deposits from the wires.

TIPS

- Pierce the hot dog so that it doesn't explode if it gets too hot.
- Blistering of the skin is a sign it's cooked.

- In the US (where 120 volts is the norm) hot dogs will take slightly longer to cook (4–6 secs).
- If you have pickles (always advisable if you're eating hot dogs), try passing a current through them and watch them glow.

LIGHT-BULB TOAST

The incandescent light bulb with its glowing filament converts just 15 per cent of the power it uses into light. The good thing about this scandalous inefficiency is that the rest is released as heat, which means that if you're using old-fashioned light bulbs you may as well cook on them.

First, find the most powerful bulb in the room. You need to suspend your raw bread above the light, so up-lighters and wall lights are ideal; all you need is something across the top to act as a grill. You can improvise, but I carry one with me, because whatever you use will get marked.

Lining the inside of the shade with foil will help reflect more heat onto your toast, and it will catch the crumbs too.

With a 60-watt bulb allow a minute per side of bread, but it all really depends on how brown you like your toast.

The surface temperature of a 100-watt bulb can reach 200–260 degrees centigrade, so don't touch!

THE IRON CHEF

A hot iron is a precision tool that allows the application of intense heat to small areas, so it's perfect for searing quick-cook meats and seafood. You'll be surprised how effective this is.

The best iron to use is the most basic model, with an entirely flat bottom and no holes, which is fortunate as they're still pretty common in hotels. If you can't find the iron, it's in the wardrobe with the laundry bags and that thing for shining your shoes.

If you're using a multi-functional modern iron with holes for steam, be extra careful to seal the food by wrapping it in foil, or grease will get into the reservoir and your collars will forever smell of bacon.

Iron-chef's bacon and eggs

This great breakfast uses the iron in both its cooking modes. For the bacon you need an ironing surface (put a towel onto the ironing board in case of greasy leaks), and for the eggs fix the iron upside down so that you can use it as a hot plate. With some models you can use the handle as a clip that slides under the ironing board or a table, holding it in place to create a ready-made hob.

What you need:

- Bacon, cut into half-size rashers
- Two eggs, lightly whisked (use a plastic fork from the restaurant)
- Tin foil – about two 15cm squares

- A tin-foil 'boat' made out of double-thickness foil, about the size of the iron's hot surface (this is going to be your cooking 'pan')
- A dash of milk (two mini servings from the tea and coffee basket will do)

What to do:

1. Heat the iron all the way up to Cotton/Linen. If there is a steam setting, switch it off!

2. Put the bacon pieces between the two squares of foil and crimp the edges so that it makes a loose bag around the bacon.

3. Press the iron onto the bacon in bursts of 20 seconds, opening one side of the foil packet every few minutes to check and allow steam to escape. Slightly crisp bacon takes about 10 minutes of ironing.

4. Put the bacon to one side.

5. Now grease inside your foil 'boat' with some of the bacon fat and place it on top of the propped-up iron.

6. Mix the milk with the eggs and pour the mixture into the boat. As the mix begins to thicken, stir or shake to make a rough omelette.

7. After about 7 minutes add the bacon, and warm it through for a further minute.

8. Serve with coffee (made the normal way in the coffee maker).

Iron-pressed toasties

The iron is really a one-sided sandwich toaster, which means the cheese toastie, or quesadilla, is the perfect hotel-room snack. Wrap your sandwich in foil (single thickness) and press with a hot iron for several minutes on each side. It's a good idea to spread a bit of mayonnaise onto the outside surface of the sandwich if you can – it helps it to go brown.

Iron-seared scallops

Season the scallops (you did get some sachets of salt and pepper from the restaurant, didn't you?). Put them between two sheets of foil and press the iron down onto the foil for 1–2 minutes per side. Prawns are a good alternative. Make sure whatever seafood you use is cooked through properly.

THE COFFEE MAKER

The filter coffee maker looks like a versatile tool for cooking. But there are drawbacks: it takes a lot of cleaning, and even then it can be hard to get rid of the coffee residue, and that's going to spoil those delicate flavours. I prefer to keep it simple and save the showy stuff for the other appliances. Even so, it can provide some useful accompaniments to the main event.

The jug

Cook in the hot water that drips through into the jug, adding your ingredients before it fills up. It's plenty warm enough to cook things like instant porridge, noodles or a boiled egg.

The basket

The filter basket makes an effective vegetable steamer. Put broccoli or finely chopped carrots into the basket and run water through the machine until your veggies are ready.

Sauces

The best way to make a sauce is in the jug. Remove the filter basket for easy access and then mix up a roux with butter and flour, gently stirring in milk and seasoning for a simple white sauce. I prefer to use the coffee machine for sweet sauces to go with a pudding. The hot plate's gentle heat is just right for meting chocolate into cream, and this way, if the coffee flavour lingers, so what? Just call it mocha.

Some people will try to convince you that you can use a coffee machine as a kind of automatic sauce maker, putting cream and lemon into the boiler, filtering it over some herbs in the basket, and letting it reduce over the hot plate to a rich goo. It's ambitious, and tempting to try it in the name of science. But please don't. It will kill the coffee machine, and your culinary ambitions with it.

THE TROUSER PRESS

It's come through some rough times, it's been the butt of countless jokes, but the trouser press has endured it all with dignity. Its tireless dedication to one simple idea deserves all of our respect, no matter how crumpled our trousers may be.

It started out in the 1930s as the 'valet stand', a glorified coat hanger, and the Corby trouser press evolved from there. Then came the 1960s, and the trouser press went electric (four years before Dylan – take that hippies!). Now, at last, the travelling salesman was free of crumpled trouser anxiety, all thanks to Corby's pin-sharp creases. The trouser press had a perfect solution for a genuine need and became the constant ally of the motorway and Travelodge fraternity from that day on.

But times changed. By the 1970s crumpled trousers were cool and the trouser press embodied everything that wasn't. But the trouser press stubbornly clung to that hotel-room wall; because deep down, hoteliers know that we love it. Like a secular Gideon's Bible, it belongs in our hotel rooms, and whether you need it or not it just feels good to know it's there.

Any trouser press is suitable for cooking, but look for models with variable temperature control and timer settings up to 45 minutes. The heat setting on most presses allows for a top cooking temperature of 60 to 80 degrees. The Corby 7700 is typical in hotels, and has all the features you'll need.

The trouser-press pancake party

The shape and size of the trouser press makes it perfect for party food – pancakes, chapattis, burritos, or whatever you call them. Better still, they come in pre-cooked packs ready to be warmed through and served.

Wrap pancakes in foil and heat for five minutes in a trouser press set to around 60. Prepare a few fillings in advance or see what you can scavenge from around the hotel.

You can fit in about five 8in pancakes at a time. If you warm them in advance, keep up to 15 pancakes in there in small stacks of three on a low heat setting. Or load a few in the press each morning, flip the switch when you get back to the room and have piping hot pancakes ready in the few minutes it takes to have a shower.

Grilled aubergine à la Corby

- Thinly sliced aubergine (about 5mm)
- Foil
- Oil and seasoning

Put the aubergine slices in foil with a good gulp of olive oil and cook for a full 45-minute cycle at 60–70 degrees.

Serving suggestion:
As a nice finishing touch put a sharp trouser-leg crease down one or two of the slices.

DIY Room Service

Menu (Half Board)

Breakfast
Coffee-maker porridge
Iron-cooked bacon and eggs served with
light-bulb toast
Tea/coffee

Dinner
Iron-seared scallops
Coffee-maker noodles with herb and lemon sauce
Slow-grilled aubergine à la trouser press
Coffee-maker-steamed broccoli florets

7.
PURELY FOR PLEASURE

*The urban bushman never lets up on his quest for adventure,
even at the weekend. Rather that zoning out while trimming
the hedge or fine tuning the catalogue of his DVD collection,
he turns to the pursuit of a special brand of bushcraft that's
purely for pleasure.*

As a kid I could shoot straight, fly a plane and punch a man with a satisfying
ker-thwack; at least until I was called in for tea. As I got older, and teatime got
later, the fantasies grew ever more grandiose. Throughout our boyhood we
play at being adults in the world of adults, with an access-all-areas pass to
the limitless universe of possibilities.

Then we grow up. But it doesn't feel like we've grown up at all. It feels more
like we've stayed the same while the world around us got boring. Our toys
are up in the attic, we're on the bus to work and our shaving rash stings like
hell. Needless to say that access-all-areas pass never materialises either. This
is the universal experience of the male human.

> **Glaswegians have a special understanding** of the impact on a man's life of having to stop playing when called in for tea. In the local patter, a mum calls in a boy playing footie on the street by yelling from the doorstep; 'yer tea's oot!' On hearing this cry, in he must go. And in a painfully perceptive leap these three words are also used by Glaswegians to evoke a more general sense of impending doom. Whether you're about to lose a fight, lose your job or lose a fortune at the hands of an online gambling consortium, it'll be the same phrase that greets you: yer tea's oot!

All the urges that got us through boyhood are still there, remodelled for the grown-up world: an obsession with lists that once had us drooling over football stickers and Top Trumps matures into a collection of Military Hardware Monthly or an outing to the local pub quiz, and the competitive rage of boyhood has to be content with a few prize begonias. What happens is that our once plentiful leisure time is repackaged, filed in a box and stored in the shed. But it doesn't have to be that way.

With a bit of guidance the urban bushman can bring playtime back into everyday life, turning his curiosity and inventiveness towards a search for grown-up kicks; the kind that can be had when using bees as an aid to urban navigation or when on an archaeological exploration down the back of the sofa. The mission is to bring back that old exuberance as we roll around in the mud and the minutiae of urban life, just for the fun of it.

ARMCHAIR ARCHAEOLOGY

The TV remote control, £3.73 in small change, an olive from last week's pizza – it all ends up down the back of the sofa. So why not enlist the whole household for an afternoon of systematic soft furnishings excavation, and create an archaeological timeline of the past few years in your living room.

This is a well-organised dig. Each person takes an armchair or sofa and begins the painstaking process of sifting and searching, dating and recording, as artefacts are uncovered and history is revealed. Build your own record of key events in the recent past as you turn up a Smartie from the top of last year's birthday cake, Grannie's reading glasses, and a small army of *Star Wars* figurines, orange pips and bits of walnut shell (from the Christmas before last, I presume).

To create your final display lay out all the finds on a length of paper (toilet roll works well) with key dates marked along a timeline. Particularly prized finds are pre-decimalisation coins, missing parts of jigsaws and card games, and the purple ones from a tin of Quality Street.

THE PAVEMENT GARDENER

Gardening doesn't have to be all about perfectly trimmed edges, gardening gloves and sprinklers. The urban bushman goes in search of his horticultural nirvana with some extreme gardening as he prepares to take on one of the most hostile terrains of the city environment, and tame it.

Herbs are tough little street fighters that can eke out a living in the meanest of streets. If you ask any gardener they'll back me up; they're always recommending herbs for the cracks in the crazy paving, so what's the difference? Let's grow a pavement herb garden.

The herbs that work best are the woodier ones (thyme, marjoram, oregano). They like it quite gritty, so the gaps between the paving stones are just right; it reminds them of the alpine nooks and crannies of home on the mountains overlooking the Med.

Start out with a few favourites outside the front door and be the first to turn the pavement into an overflow herb garden. Some of them will go into the pot, others will release their fragrance as you pass and crush scented leaves underfoot.

Next you can start to cultivate a colony or two on some more distant parts of your daily route; outside the newsagents or beside the bus stop. Places where pavings have been recently removed for cable laying or pipe maintenance are particularly fertile, as are stretches habituated by dog walkers.

DEATH TO THE BARBECUE

Put down those tongs and step away from the barbecue. You've got bigger things on your mind.

For urban man the sight of food browning over the embers is a repeat showing of his finest hour; a reminder of how he controlled one of nature's most terrifying forces and how it made him feel like king. So it makes sense that where there's a barbecue, there's always a man presiding over the burst sausages, and he won't surrender those tongs without a struggle; this polite little ritual of briquettes and bangers is as close as he gets these days to satisfying his primal need. But why settle for this substitute when you can have the real thing?

When man cooks he wants people to take notice, he wants flames, and he wants to leave great big scorch marks on the earth . . . Get ready for the Chicken Inferno.

CHICKEN INFERNO

A golden-brown rotisserie chicken, ready in 15 minutes of blazing glory!

Cooking in unusual ways on unconventional cookers is one method to turn food preparation into an adventure with man appeal. The other way is to make it big and make it spectacular, because when a man cooks he instinctively wants people to take notice.

This chicken recipe is my once-a-year dose of adrenaline cookery that has the right mix of mischief and theatre to keep me going until the following summer. It's particularly effective after dark.

What you need:

- A bale of hay/straw, tinder dry
- A cleaned metal canister/drum, about 20–30 litres*
- A large bottle, clean
- One chicken
- Marinade ingredients
- A large fireproof dish
- Oven gloves

How it works

Your chicken is going to be flash roasted in the centre of an inferno of hay.

For ten minutes or so you'll have a roaring fire to gawp at, and five minutes later you'll be serving a beautifully cooked chicken to some pretty impressed guests.

Preparation

With a sharp knife gently score the chicken down to the bone, in strips of about 2cm, so that it all cooks evenly. Now marinade it for at least two hours in a spicy barbecue blend, rubbing the oily mixture in well.

While the chicken's marinating, clean the canister thoroughly and cut off one end with a hacksaw or angle grinder.

Now find an open space where you can safely set light to your mini haystack, and prepare your guests for the big moment.

* A catering-sized cooking-oil drum would be perfect.

Instructions

- Put the neck of the bottle into the chicken cavity so that the chicken perches on the neck and the bottle. Stand the bottle on the dish to collect the gravy. Gently place the canister over the chicken so that it doesn't touch, and cover the whole thing with hay in a pyramid shape to make a tightly pressed mini haystack.
- Fifteen minutes before you want to serve, set light to the hay and stand back!
- Let the fire burn naturally and listen out for the chicken sizzling inside. Leave the embers to carry on cooking the bird after the flames have died down.
- Once the embers have died brush away the ashes without disturbing the canister. Maybe put a big stone on top to stop it moving while you clear the hay.
- Carefully lift off the canister (it will still be very hot) to reveal your roast chicken and delicious bowl of gravy.

As with any roast chicken, prod the meatiest part with a skewer to make sure it's cooked all the way through. If the juices don't run clear, give it another five-minute blast. Your guests are unlikely to object.

MUSSEL MEN

In Britain we think of the barbecue as suburban man's great caveman moment. But it pales beside the pumped-up outdoor cookery that men get away with all over the world. A few summers ago in a corner of France where mussels are big business I was asked along to a 'fête' with a barbecue in the square. When I got there, five or six men were prodding a bonfire with pitchforks, arranging the blazing logs into a base onto which went a cooking pot the size of a cattle trough. Next, a truckload of mussels arrived, to be transferred to the pot by wheelbarrow, and the final ingredient was a bathtub of tomato sauce, all stirred by spade.

That's what I call man-sized catering. The approach was the same as if they'd been putting up a marquee or towing a tractor out of a ditch: there was a job to be done. This wasn't about pretensions to *haute cuisine*; it was a celebration of the untamed delights of good food and full bellies. When the mussels were served, nobody was commenting on the presentation or quibbling about the seasoning. Food like this demands to be devoured, and it was. I'll take one night like that over any number of summer evenings prodding the charcoal briquettes.

NAVIGATING WITH CITY BEES

Navigating without a map is a bushcraft perennial, but it's not often you get the chance to recruit an insect to help do away with the A–Z. All you need is a bit of help from a local beekeeper and you're away. First came GPS, now here's BeePS.

Bees and beekeepers are no strangers to the city,* and producing urban honey is the new hobby to have.** This happy fact allows the urban bushman to borrow a technique from the honey hunters of the rainforest and turn it into one of the most adventurous days out the suburbs can offer.

In the jungle, honey is a rare delicacy and the sweet-toothed tribesmen have become expert in pinpointing bee hives. The simple principle is to catch bees, then release them and follow them back to the hive. It can be as simple as that, but bees are hard to follow, so you may end up with terrible

* There are over 2000 beekeepers within London's M25 orbital motorway.
** Urban honey bees produce more honey than rural bees and seem to be unaffected by environmental pollution. Some producers claim urban honey is more pure because pollen from city gardens hasn't been sprayed with pesticides.

eye strain and very little chance of honey. Consequently, the tribesmen do something very clever: a bit of basic triangulation. This is the system now removed from the primary rainforest and reinvented for the urban conurbation.

THE BASIC IDEA

The system works best with three or more people. One of you has to collect the bees and deliver them to the others, who have each picked a different spot within a three-mile radius of the hive. Each participant will then have a container housing a few bees but no idea where the hive is located. Their challenge is to use the bees to guide them in, and the first one to the hive is the winner.

In my ideal world this sort of thing would be a basic entry test for MI5: here are your bees, now find your way back to base.

What you need:
- *Bees*: (five to ten) for each person, in a suitable container. Try asking your friendly beekeeper to do this bit.
- *A picnic*: come on, make a day of it.

How it works

Bees are great navigators and can find their hive from anywhere in a 5km (3-mile) radius. They tend to fly up in a circling motion, and as soon as they have a fix on where they are, they make a 'beeline' for home. They navigate by using the angle of the sun, but they're also thought to spot familiar landmarks like motorways and big buildings, so look out for appropriate sights around your chosen start point.

To find the hive, first release one bee, watch it closely and take a rough bearing on its eventual direction (towards the tower block, to the left of the gas works, that sort of thing). Now imagine a line at roughly 90 degrees to the bee's direction and pick a spot about a kilometre (half a mile) away on that line. That's where you should release your next bee. Then repeat the process once more.

Warning: If there's any possibility that you may have an allergy to bee stings, this is not for you.

Urban bushcraft icon Sir Francis Galton spotted a version of this technique on his various adventures in Africa, and it obviously appealed to him too, as it merited inclusion in his explorers' guide book, *The Art of Travel:* 'Honey, to find, when bees are about: – Catch a bee, tie a feather or straw to its leg, which can easily be done (natives thrust it up into its body), and follow him as he flies slowly to his hive.'

Now this is where the triangulation comes in. Plot your bees' courses and where they cross should be the location of the hive. It won't be precise, but if you've got a few bees left, try again when you get nearer.

Urban bushcraft through the ages: John Steinbeck

Steinbeck had worked as a farm hand, a war correspondent and a handyman at a ski resort before he wrote *The Grapes of Wrath*, won the Pulitzer Prize and became a full-time literary icon. But to me his great legacy is the art-form he created in a few hours of down time in 1960.

This was the year he decided to tour the USA in a camper van with his poodle, Charlie. A few months into it, Steinbeck wanted a break, so he booked a hotel while Charlie went to a poodle parlour (all true, I swear). Anyway, he showed up before his room was ready but there was one available, and though that one hadn't been cleaned, Steinbeck took it while he waited.

To most of us this would have been an unpleasant hour in a dirty hotel room, tiptoeing around somebody else's leavings. Yuk. But Steinbeck didn't see it like that. He tuned into something profound. Looking around the room at the fragments of its previous occupant's life he felt a natural instinct take over. He was receiving a primal signal, picking up an image of the man who'd been there a few hours before.

The legendary trackers of the Wild West could paint detailed pictures of their quarry by looking at a few broken twigs and some half-covered tracks. Now Steinbeck was carrying on where they left off, reacting to the clues he could read, as an urban tracker: an empty whiskey bottle, laundry tickets, an unfinished letter in the bin. He built an entire profile of the guest and his previous 24 hours and even gave the guy a name. 'As I sat in this unmade room, Lonesome Harry began to take shape and dimension,' he wrote later.

We do this all the time; judging people by the space they inhabit. And we expect others to do the same in relation to us. We tidy our desk or our bedroom before a visitor calls; we leave the right books on show and hide the wrong ones. Steinbeck recognised this innate awareness and gave it dignity. Urban tracking had found its voice. Not bad for a few hours in a dirty hotel room.

SIR FRANCIS GALTON'S SEASIDE SNOOZE PIT

A day on the beach is as close as many of us ever get to a wilderness adventure. As leader of the expedition we're called on to make a series of decisions from the off: how much kit to transport (whether to leave the windbreak in the car), selecting a route (across the dunes or via the firm wet stuff near the sea) and finding a suitable spot to camp (close to the ice cream vans and crowds or that patch of space near the headland?).

In the interest of morale a bit of give and take is inevitable; this is the burden of all expedition leaders. But the urban bushman consoles himself with a pet project on which compromise is totally out of the question; digging his personal snooze pit.

As the leader of several scientific forays across Africa, Victorian explorer and polymath Sir Francis Galton was familiar with the pressure on an expedition leader and understood the need for comfortable rest. When it came to preparing the ground on which he would sleep, Galton spoke from bitter experience when he wrote; *'It is disagreeable enough to lie on a perfectly level surface like that of a floor, but the acme of discomfort is to lie upon a convexity.'* Ah Sir Francis, you're so right.

By convexity he meant a bump, of course. And nobody likes to sleep on a bump. But it's the next step that's crucial. Instead of a convexity you hollow out a human-shaped dip, or in Galton's language, a concavity.

The important thing here is to remember that humans aren't flat sided. Imagine the shape of the dip in your mattress when you're asleep, and replicate that in the sand.

Preparing a seaside snooze pit (adapted from Sir Francis Galton's The Art of Travel*)*

1. Remove any stones or other debris.
2. Scrape a hollow, deepest at the point of the hips and accommodating the shoulders.

3. Lay in it your rug or mat.

4. Lay on top of the rug so that your hips and shoulders fit the contours.

5. Commence snoozing.

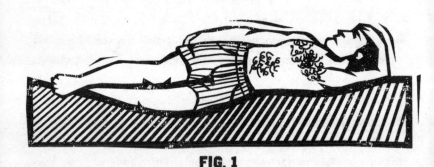

FIG. 1

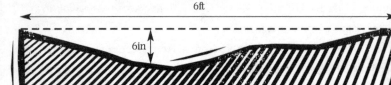

FIG. 2

This project appeals to the obsessive mind of the urban bushman; it takes several tries to get it right and there's always room for improvement. Galton, of course, took this incredibly seriously and included a calculation of the perfect shape of a sleeping 'lair'. For a 6ft man he calculated that the perfect 'concavity' should be six inches at its deepest and of the shape shown in the diagram.

120: THE SECRET TO MOBILE PHONE HAPPINESS

The urban bushman is a primate who uses a mobile and shares 96 per cent of his genetic material with apes who don't. Although our cousins are behind on predictive text and speed dial, they can show us the perfect number of contacts to store in our phones.

You're on the train and bored with your book; what do you do? Instead of switching on your brain, you get out your phone for some idle flicking through the functions. You browse through the names stored in the memory, either looking for someone to call, or weeding out any who deserve to be deleted, then erasing them with satisfaction.

I know I'm not the only one who grooms the contacts in my phone like this. The list represents our unique social network and we're the hub. Nobody else has a list like it, so it's natural that we're taken with it and enjoy the occasional stroll in its company. But that cosy feeling is hiding some serious science.

120 IS PLENTY

Anthropologists spotted long ago that primitive settlements of people don't grow a lot bigger than 120, and when they do they split apart. Just as 120 was the upper limit for tight-knit communities in Neolithic settlements long ago, so it is in the villages of developing countries today.

How many weddings have you been to when the guests numbered around 120? How many business conferences hand out roughly that many name badges? When you start looking, the figure 120 is everywhere. It's a scout hut at parade time, a well-filled village hall, a packed restaurant; in other words, we seem to know that 120 is just enough.

And apart from weddings and business meetings there's another place where the spirit of the primitive village lives on; in our phones, of course. If you've held back so far, don't wait any longer. Count the numbers stored in your mobile and there's a good chance you'll get to around 120. If you're over, I bet there are a few you could delete without ever missing them.

> **I was taught at school** that the basic unit that built the Roman Army was a century, 100 men. But that was only after the reforms of Marius in about 100 BC. Before then, in its heyday, the Roman Army had something else instead; the maniple, a fighting unit of 120–130 men.

PRIMATES AND 150

But surely there's no harm in letting our contacts list grow and grow, you may say. This is where the apes come in, and here to introduce them is Robin Dunbar, an Oxford anthropologist.

Dunbar studies social circles in apes. And he tells us that if you're in an ape clique you get groomed on a regular basis; if you aren't, you don't. He noticed that the number of apes in any social circle was always pretty similar. Then he had his big idea: what if the thing that limits the number of social contacts is brain space? To Dunbar it was obvious: to form any meaningful bond, one primate needs to know another primate's entire background, how they fit in and who else they're connected with, and that's a lot of data to cram into a brain the size of a grapefruit.

Like all anthropologists, Dunbar was keen to point out that we're apes and that we go in for grooming too. Apes take it literally, squishing the ticks and fleas in each other's fur. We find other ways to get close to each other, like offering lifts in the car, sharing meals or sitting next to each other at the pictures. And the number of people we allow to get that close is our grooming clique.

So next Dunbar took that number of the average ape clique, and the average human clique and compared their size. Then he looked at the difference in size between an ape brain (a grapefruit), and our human brains (a honeydew melon). And guess what – the difference was the same. Our social group was bigger in proportion to the bigger size of our brain. From that moment on the upper limit of a human social group has been known as Dunbar's Number. What is the number? It's 150 (in fact it was 148, but he rounded it up, which I find likeably casual of him).

To anthropologists, 150 seemed close enough to 120 for the difference not really to matter. And that sounds like a worrying leap for our theory about mobile phones. After all 30 extra names is a lot to account for on anyone's contacts list ... But closer inspection of Dunbar's definition of this social group reveals the badly needed loophole. His circle of 150 contacts includes old buddies we've lost touch with but could easily pick up with again because we still have all that valuable data. The social bond is strong, just dormant. In other words, we remember them, but we don't have their phone number!

So if you deduct 30 to cover all those we've lost touch with, the magic 120 lives on. And we now understand why it's important to keep clearing out the phone memory too. More than 120 means brain strain, it just feels wrong. The phone could store far more, but what's the point? We'd never call them and we know it. They just don't belong.

THE FACEBOOK PROOF

The mobile is a constant companion and we prefer it to mirror the capacity of our brains, not to add to it like some kind of plug-in hard drive. But what about online networking sites like Facebook? Dunbar predicted they could be the end of his magic number. These sites are all about acquiring 'friends' who can send their profile with a click, allowing us to boost our circle of friends exponentially, without unlimited RAM.

Well, in early 2009 *The Economist* magazine asked Facebook to crunch some numbers and tell them on average how many 'friends' each Facebook user has. And Facebook came up with an answer that seems too good to be true. It was 120. This is all very reassuring for anyone who likes to think that friendship is about more than data storage. Despite the runaway potential of new technology the primate brain holds sway.

120: as a darts score it's not bad, but as an address list it's perfect.

THINGS TO DO IN STARBUCKS

Use your Starbucks state of mind to reconnect with a more resourceful past . . .

The low lighting, the comfy seats and those subtle shades of brown are working overtime to make you feel at home and buy another latte. And it's effective, you have to admit. Of course, you're right not to be taken in by the folksy logo and the green aprons; there's nothing homespun about Starbucks at all. But what fascinates me is that the story being sold here is so seductive. It's all about nostalgia, wafting us on a cloud of butterscotch froth back to a time when life was simple, time was plentiful and coffee cost much less than £2 a hit. It's artfully done, and it took millions of dollars of venture capital to pull it off, so you may as well make good use of it . . .

STIRRER STAR RACE

Time: ten minutes

The sticks that are used to stir coffee may look like lolly sticks, but they have a critical difference: extra flexibility. This is what makes it possible to construct the star below, all held together with nothing but friction. If making Christmas decorations isn't your thing, you can always reinvent them as Kung Fu death stars.

Have a race to see who can make one first, starting with the simplest five-stick model. This is what you should end up with:

Other stirrer art projects could include: Wicker Man, moon lander, stick insect.

LATTE LINGO BINGO

For two players or more.

Here's a sample bingo card; I'm sure you can work it out for yourself from here.

SKINNY	SHOT	VENTI	CHAI
LATTE	GRANDE	CAPPUCINO	VERY BERRY

FROTHY PERSONALITIES PREDICTOR

At busy times this works especially well. You need a seat near the service area. The aim is to predict what drink each person in the queue is going to buy, and it's uncanny how easy it is to get this right. A good variation of the game is to take turns to guess the drink, and the size of cup of each order. An online application called Starbucks Oracle gives each Starbucks drink a corresponding personality type. Look it up if you must. In this game you just use your instinctive knowledge of these fairly obvious associations. Sometimes you can look at someone and you just know they're a skinny decaff frappuccino.

THREE THINGS YOU DIDN'T KNOW ABOUT STARBUCKS

THERE IS A SMALL SIZE

They don't advertise it on the menu, but it's on the pricing structure, and the staff all know about it. Ask for a 'short' (of course they wouldn't call it 'small'). The actual size (8oz) is a third smaller than the next smallest ('tall'), but with the same single shot. Cappuccino connoisseurs will recognise immediately that this is much closer to the Italian way of making the drink – maximum coffee, minimum froth.

THE FOAM HAT TRICK

On a cold day ask for extra foam on top of your takeaway coffee. It keeps it warm, like a woolly hat.

'THAT'S GROSS, DUDE'

Starbucks baristas on a US staff blog compare notes on their most disgusting drink orders. Last time I looked, the winner was something called a 'triple grande pomegranate fruit juice frappuccino'.

8.
THE FUTURE

Urban bushcraft kicks against the idea that progress has to be one way. If the clock went into reverse, just imagine what you'd discover. Life would be one long re-learning curve. At the start you'd find out how we really did manage without mobile phones, and by the end you'd know how to build your own pyramid.

A lot of what we call bushcraft, urban or otherwise, comes from this resourceful past. In compiling this book it's been my pleasure to watch some fairly rustic survival skills take off their muddy boots and help out around the modern home, or come blundering into town and adapt to the modern city.

But the urban bushman has another greater source of knowledge, and we're only just beginning to tap into its riches. I'm talking about the wisdom of the great urban tribesmen. I call it urban lore and it comes from those special people in our cities who are supremely adapted to their habitat.

It's people like *Big Issue* sellers, taxi drivers, estate agents and supermarket security guards. Like the bushmen of the Kalahari, they'd be pretty useless anywhere else, but on their home patch they're unbeatable. The true urban bushman mingles with these master practitioners, studies their behaviour, and considers it an honour to preserve their skills for future generations.

The long-distance truck driver instinctively knows the best place to stop for a pee on the A74M southbound when you've just gone past Gretna Green.* The ticket tout gleans enough information about you from a moment's eye contact to fill an encyclopaedia. And the corner-shop owner has developed the ability to tell a genuine shopper from a pie snatcher or a chocolate thief. As well as that, his instinct tells him the right number of schoolchildren to allow into the shop at any one time.

These ancient oral traditions are passed down from father to son in wisdom encoded into their culture. It's the urban bushman's duty to preserve as many of their skills and secrets as he can, for a brighter future. We either use it, or lose it.

* It's the Todhills rest area just after junction 44.

INDEX